LOVE, LOSS &
LONELINESS

'It's not easy to write about suffering and loss. This book manages to blend raw honesty with realistic hope in a richly helpful way.'

Revd Canon J. John, speaker, writer and
Director of The Philo Trust

'I was very impressed with the reality streaked throughout *Love, Loss & Loneliness*. It was painful to read and helpful to read, and if you can achieve that in one book you've done a mighty thing.'

Revd Dr Russ Parker, director of
Healing Wounded Churches, author and speaker

'*Love, Loss and Loneliness* is one of those very rare books that addresses the sometimes harsh and harrowing realities of life in a hopeful and healing way. Looking specifically at bereavement, Nick Battle tells the true stories of those who have entered the very heart of grief's darkness and found heaven's light. This book is a life-giving resource for anyone travelling the hard road of bereavement. Prepare to be moved and inspired.'

Dr Mark Stibbe, author and
CEO of Kingdom Writing Solutions

LOVE, LOSS & LONELINESS

A companion in grief

NICK BATTLE

Authentic

21 20 19 18 17 16 15   7 6 5 4 3 2 1

First published 2015 by Authentic Media Limited
52 Presley Way, Crownhill, Milton Keynes, MK8 0ES.
authenticmedia.co.uk

British Library Cataloguing in Publication Data
A catalogue record for this book is available from the British Library.
ISBN: 978-1-78078-232-4   978-1-78078-233-1 (e-book)

Cover design by Peter Barnsley creativehoot.com
Author photo by Tony Swain
Printed by Kingsbridge Press Ltd., Northern Ireland

This book is dedicated to my friend and
father-in-law Phil Edwards

Acknowledgements

Thank you to Malcolm Down who saw the need for a book like this when others didn't. It's good to have you in my corner.

Thank you to the trustees of the Gravel Road Trust, past and present, and to our patrons for standing up for those suffering loss and loneliness.

To my children Misha and Jodie who had to endure their own journey and with whom I am so very blessed to have such a wonderful and close relationship. You know how very proud I am of you both.

And finally, thank you to my wife Nicky who, by the grace of God, enabled a new beginning and in so doing gave me our son Jesse. What great joy! Thank you for the last ten years. I look forward to all that remains in our life together.

To God be the glory.

Contents

PART I
LIFE LESSONS

Introduction

Hope Mountain

How do you start to write a book titled, *Love, Loss & Loneliness*? Each word is so full of meaning that I'm reluctant even to begin. The truth is this book was originally titled *Good Grief*, until someone else used that for a title and I realized that however neat a phrase that is, it oversimplifies a very complex process. We can try to wrest some positives out of our experience of loss, and indeed should, but that doesn't mean that grief itself is good. What you make of it and how you respond to it may be good, but grief itself is not a positive but a negative reality. So while I do not pretend to have all the bases covered when it comes to love, loss and loneliness, I don't want to be trite. I simply want to share some of the lessons I have learnt that may be of help. That has been my motivation for writing this book.

As I've responded to my own loss, and faced that loss in the process of writing, I have had to grapple with questions that all of us ask in the uphill struggle of dealing with grief.

Did God create the three conditions of love, loss and loneliness?

Or does he simply allow them to happen?

Does he understand them?

And why does he allow them to persist?

Why doesn't he intervene?

I don't know.

What I do know is that God – or whoever or whatever you might wish to call him – is right there with us in the mess, holding our hand as we walk through the valley of the shadow of despair to begin the long and winding road to the summit of a mountain called Hope.

He may come to you in the guise of a consistent friend or a concerned colleague. He may come to you in your dreams at night or through the unconditional kindness of a stranger. He may come to you through what may feel to you like barren, empty prayers and mere rhetoric. However he comes, know that he is there. It is just that from time to time we forget.

All of us, at moments in our lives, find ourselves straining every sinew to climb the mountain of Hope. At times hope has been all I have had. Just the tiniest chink of light can provide it. And when you're in the midst of a coal-black night, blindly stumbling around, it is when the light momentarily penetrates your darkness that you dare even for a second to dream again.

So never lose hope. At some point, life has to get better.

Onwards!

Upwards!

1

A Ball of Tangled String

As the 1980s songwriter Howard Jones put it so adroitly, 'What Is Love Anyway?'

Since the dawn of time men and women have needed love – from the Garden of Eden to programmes like *I'm a Celebrity Get Me Out of Here* (which on more than one occasion has documented, sometimes in graphic detail, people's need for relationship). Everybody needs love. We were made to be together – man and woman, like a hand in a glove.

In an ideal world (which seems less likely than ever to exist today), you fall in love, commit to getting married, you make love and then somewhere down the line, God willing, you have a child together. That's how God designed it, right? It's a nice thought, isn't it, but perhaps a little old-fashioned. Today we live in a world where you can choose to have a stranger's embryo implanted in your womb and where same sex couples can have a family by adoption or surrogacy. Is this what God had in mind when he created Adam and Eve? Or should that be Adam and Steve? I don't know. I have friends of both sexes and family members who are gay and/or 'exploring' their sexuality. I refuse to judge them or anybody else for that matter, for the simple reason that I know I have no right to.

Christians have been far too quick to leap on bandwagons, whether it's the one labelled 'Divorce' in the 1970s, or the one labelled 'Gay' at the beginning of this century. In so doing they heap a whole world of pain on people who may or may not be in a relationship with God but who are on a journey and who far too often feel ostracized as a result of these unkind dismissals.

If you're reading this book and that has happened to you, I want to apologize.

It's not what Jesus would have done.

Love and pain

What is love?

It's a bit like this: we have each been given a huge ball of string and, somehow, over the course of our lives we get to try to unravel it. Some of us will get very tangled up and feel bound by what we have or have not done. Others will cut through it like a hot knife through butter. Some may appear to have it all neatly sewn up, at least from the outside.

The bottom line though is this: if you want to really experience love, then you must get acquainted with its intimate bedfellow, *pain*.

I truly fell in love for the first time when I was 22. There had been girls before, and even an engagement, but I didn't have a clue what love was. Love had never been modelled for me by my mum and dad. In fact quite the reverse was true. So I stumbled around bumping into girls and I hurt a lot of people in the process.

My first love was someone I'd known for a while – a friend who was elegant, smart, graceful and beautiful. She knew what she wanted, and one night, after a bunch of friends came back home with me from the pub, she marched right into the kitchen where I was making tea for everybody and kissed me on the lips. It was a spectacular kiss, one that hinted at a reservoir of as yet undiscovered pleasure.

My young body and mind now felt overwhelmed with desire for this bold young woman who had kissed me so firmly in my mother's house. Over the months – and oh so short year and a half (on and off) – I fell for her as deeply as my limited experience would allow. It was love. But not as I now know it. She became my oxygen. My desire to be with her became insatiable. I hated being away from her. I ached for her. My heart and soul cried out for her presence 24/7. I was drunk with longing.

With the benefit of hindsight I can see that she, on the other hand, felt claustrophobic, and understandably so. I had no experience of stability, while she came from a very secure and loving home with strong, glamorous and successful parents. She took a holiday in America, and when she came back she was never really present in the same way again. She had learnt how to fly.

Throughout my twenties I barrelled my way through relationships in search of that same feeling. I came close but, as they say, no cigar. By the time I hit my thirties all my friends were married, some even had children. Meanwhile I was slowly blurring the lines between friends who were girls and 'girlfriends'. The truth was I was clueless. Until, that is, I met the one.

I loved her so much I married her.

We had two children and were soul mates until the day, thirteen and a half years later, cancer robbed her of her final breath.

What is love?

That was.

Love and loss

I understand loss quite well. My parents' marriage had imploded in the 1970s and I was all too aware of what it felt like to live with the fallout of that, which perhaps explains why it took me so very long to get married. That we were able to sustain such a happy relationship for so long says a lot about my wife's patience, loyalty and grace, and perhaps the fact that over the years I, too, may have just learnt a lesson or two about love.

The loneliness had always been there. Dad was absent and Mum drank, so I retreated to the two common denominators that have served me so well at each stage in my life: faith and music. Even now they remain my default settings. But nothing prepares you for losing your soul mate. The day I finally said goodbye is one that is carved on my heart forever.

The day the dream died.

The 'til death us do part.

The happy ever after.

The forsaking all others.

Just the two of us.

'You and me against the world kid.'

That was the loneliest day of my life.

Since then, eleven years on, I have discovered more about love, loss and loneliness, which is why I finally now feel ready to try to write from my perspective about the whole shooting match.

Love and grieving

Just when do we start grieving? How should we? Who do we feel safe enough to grieve with? How does it manifest itself? For some people grieving is a complex and intricate process, while for others it seems, on the surface, to be an altogether easier reality.

There are many different experiences of grief. You can grieve as a carer or as somebody who has been bereaved, but what about the patient diagnosed with a life-threatening illness? What do they grieve? Is it their mortality and their lost opportunities?

My late wife used to say, 'You lose me, but I lose all of you . . .'

You see, it's all loss. We are in a sense, 'losing' from the day we are born.

But maybe we can find a way of 'winning'.

For those of us who are left behind and have had to release loved ones into the arms of Jesus, we have to let go and we have to let God. That has been, and sometimes continues to be, a severe mercy. From time to time we may get ambushed emotionally and often spiritually. But how can we take what has happened and turn it to good?

C.S. Lewis said, and I paraphrase here, 'Do not waste your sorrows.' So we have to learn to take the tears of sadness and soak the foot of the cross with them. At times that's all we can do, weep at Jesus' feet. But then, like a baby taking its first steps we learn to walk again, falteringly at first, but slowly faith builds and our friends and family, church and community, sow kindness into our lives, as do others who travel a similar and yet unique and individual path.

Then we learn to hope again and our heart that once wanted to stop, just as our loved one's did, now starts to beat to a more regular and intrinsic rhythm and we start to dance again to the choreography of the Holy Spirit.

And we realize in all this sadness that God is still God – bigger than breath, life-giving and life-taking.

So we walk with a little more grace and a lot more gratitude for what we have than we did before, and we love harder and deeper – for we know it is not for ever. We look to the bold promise of heaven and sometimes can't wait to get there, and it is with that ache that we begin to win, or even know that we *have* won.

Love and God

Is there ever such a thing as 'good grief'? Does such a thing exist? Surely this phrase is an oxymoron if ever there was one. It is very complicated and a highly individual process. Sitting here, typing these words eleven years down the road from losing my first wife, it seems at first a preposterous concept. But then I believe that in the working out of my bereavement, it's a phrase which describes where I've come to.

Would I have chosen the pain of 'searing loss', of having my heart ripped from my chest and cleft in two, and having to watch my daughters' anguish as I manage my own? No. But it's what life dealt me. Bad stuff happens. How we respond to it, that's what really matters. This is how we win.

But we don't win on our own. It's all down to God. He is love. He invented it. It's who he is. It's what he does. So in our own frail attempts at loving, we can ask him to help us to do it well. We can lift our hands to heaven and implore him to help us when we lose someone we love. In other words, we can pray – even if it doesn't always feel like he is listening.

In the days after my wife died, God answered in the form of people's kindness, phone calls, letters and emails. I was overwhelmed by that. Two close friends took over all the funeral arrangements: from the delicate removal of the body of my wife to the procession into church to the Waterboys' song 'The Whole of the Moon', right up to the, oh so very final, laying of her beautiful mortal earthly self in the grounds of the church where we were so happily married thirteen and a half years earlier.

He was there.

He understands.

He is love.

Love and time

I said thirteen and a half years. That *half* is important. One of the many earthly things you yearn for when someone is dying is more time. And yet there is an irony here because you want their pain – and if I'm really honest, your own – to stop, to come to a full stop. You want them to stop hurting. And I'm not talking just about physical pain, which can be immense, but the pain of a person's psyche torn by subtle and insidious doubts, manifested in late night conversations that fly around your head accompanied by all those if onlys.

Oh yes, there are a million and one ways to have your heart broken. We all get to chew on that chilli at some point. But for some of us it just comes earlier rather than later. Sooner or later the sands of time run out and this is where the stuff hits the fan or, to use a phrase from more polite and anodyne circles, where the rubber hits the road.

Do you think you've got more courage than most?

Try staring death down over a ten-year period.

That's a long time.

But my sweet Lord, that is just what my wife did. God alone knows just what she endured, or how.

As her husband I got to share in some of it and I would say this: it was and remains a privilege.

Do I think I could have handled things better? Definitely, but that's my stuff, my modus operandi, my baggage. Call it what you like. It's my business.

I've learnt things though – about myself, about people, about God. So I'm going to try to unravel it and hope that within my messy ball of string, you perhaps get to untie a few knots as well and maybe realize that it's not all loss. And that, as an old friend of mine once wrote, 'There's a bright tomorrow just around the corner.'

We just have to make it through the rain.

2

Grinding out the Grief Miles

I remember waking up in front of the fire with my dog Max cradled in my arms. It had just turned five o'clock in the morning. And then it hit me. Lynn was gone.

It seemed impossible that such a vital life force could leave our planet. Even the night before, when she gently tried to tell me all the things she would like taken care of, it never occurred to me that Lynn would die the following day. Of course I knew that she was very seriously ill, but she had been at death's door before and had always managed to beat it one way or the other. She was the, 'Comeback Kid', only this time she had not come back, and I was swimming in a giant ocean of grief where the waves come crashing down on you, relentless and unforgiving.

The quantity of flowers that arrived was bizarre. Why do we send flowers when someone has died? It's not like the departed can enjoy them. Our lounge looked like the window of a florist's shop.

Of much greater value were the letters and cards my children and I received from people who wrote with great love and tenderness. Those messages, along with the Book of Condolence, I keep to this day. They remain the bright remnants of a life well lived – a life greatly loved.

Starting the journey

The days immediately after seemed to float by in a pain-filled blur: I'd catch the scent of Lynn's perfume as I opened the wardrobe door; I'd look in the mirror and expect to see her standing behind me.

My dog Max scratched a patch of skin two inches in diameter absolutely red raw. He was literally and intuitively feeling our pain. For the last six months of Lynn's life he had sneaked upstairs (where he wasn't allowed) to lie by the side of her bed.

My father and his wife turned up and stayed for two weeks, which was immensely helpful until they left. Then once again the children and I felt bereft.

But this was important. There comes a point where we have to be left alone to try to find a way forward. It is hard, very hard, but it must be done. It can be made easier if you know you can pick up the phone to someone, comforted that help is not far away. It is during these days that you really begin to grind out the grief miles and find out who your real friends are.

Some medical practitioners recommend counselling to help the process. In our case, this happened far too soon. It was done by someone who meant well, but it just served to stir up our grief even more and wasn't helpful. If you have a broken leg and the plaster has just set, why would you want to rip the plaster off, re-examine the fracture and in so doing perhaps add to the pain before wrapping it up once again, hoping it will mend? It doesn't make sense. Although this may not necessarily be the case for everyone, as a general rule time should be allowed to pass before this delicate process of counselling should be attempted.

In our situation, none of what was happening felt real. It just hurt terribly. I had a hole in my heart and I felt it could never, ever, be filled.

Lost innocence

Do you remember your first kiss? And all the other kisses with people in between until you met 'The One'?

I could say that as a young man I both enjoyed and endured countless relationships, but that is not strictly accurate. Let's just say I broke a few hearts and had mine broken too.

In the 1970s and 1980s, the young alpha male represented not so much a knight in shining armour, as a night on the tiles. I was barrelling through life at 150 mph, not really caring for anyone apart from myself. I'm sure I caused a lot of pain for some, which I deeply regret. Actually, I probably caused more to myself. That sounds pretty selfish doesn't it? It could all have been so much better. I do regret hurting people and breaking hearts.

I also grieve over my loss of trust, about the systematic erosion of my belief as a child that all was right with the world, that Mummy and Daddy were happy – despite the fact that she drank until she passed out in the turquoise velour swivel chair, and he only came home at the weekends to the

G-Plan-teak world that we euphemistically called 'home'. I would often find my mother's false teeth and panty-girdle stuffed underneath a cushion the morning after, as if she'd wanted to get comfortable before drowning her sorrows. Her cloud of sadness followed her around like a faithful puppy in need of obedience classes.

Did the alcohol and prescription drugs help her with the grief caused by the breakup of her marriage to my father?

No.

Looking back on my childhood I grieve most of all for lost opportunities, for the fact that I started to parent my mum at the age of 13, when I began to understand just how much damage she was doing to herself.

I am upset because mine was not a happy home but a cauldron of inglorious dysfunction, a place where my mother professed a faith in God but blasphemed often and loudly – although only ever at home. There was an irony here. On the one hand she liked the 'High' church of the Anglicans, with all their bells and smells, and would genuflect before the cross of her Saviour. On the other hand she endured a life of extreme melancholy. These seemed at odds with one another.

If Jesus was all he was supposed to be, why wasn't Mum happier?

I lost my innocent view of life the first time my mother tried to take her life.

It was on a Christmas day morning in Manchester. There was just me, my dear blind nana, and the kind paramedics. Life was clearly not the exciting journey I had thought.

But what broke me even more than this was years later, walking alongside my daughters as they came to understand just how desperately ill their mummy was and that she was going to die.

They were just nine and ten.

When they learnt that awful truth, they didn't just lose their innocence, they lost their whole world.

Where is the good in that?

After the funeral

There were initially three journeys down the gravel road of grief after Lynn died – my own and those of my two lovely daughters. But it quickly became more complex than that, as our emotions spilled out and over each other – at times so quickly and with such force that it was like someone had put our three hearts in the blender and turned it on to maximum power with the lid not on properly.

What happens after all the fuss has died down and your loved one has been laid to rest?

So you've had all the intensity of the funeral and been overwhelmed by loss but you've also been consumed by the emotions of other people coming in and out of your house and your heart – well-meaning friends who just can't help but leave their steaming pile of emotional excrement on the carpet before exiting stage left, weeping.

For these lovely and well-meaning people, you need shed-loads of grace.

Dewey-eyed over 'what might have been' and 'how much she meant to me', their response is sincere and heartfelt in their own minds. But if she meant that much, why didn't they see her more often? How we need grace with such people. I call them the 'Erstwhiles'.

Then there are the old friends from university, college or early working life who turn up to honour the deceased, say beautiful things at the funeral, and then abruptly vanish into thin air. I call these the 'Thrushes'. They mean well but their absence is irritating.

Then there are the 'Stoics'. These comprise a small band of people who have known you both. They have loved the deceased as well as you and the rest of the family. They will stand by you and help you grind out the miles. Their love and role in your life and the lives of your immediate family is incalculable. They are rarer than hen's teeth and to be prized at all times.

Finally there are the 'Newbies'. These are people who come into your life knowing not much about the past but actively choosing to befriend you. They will invest time, love, and energy into your life. These people, along with the Stoics, are God's manna from heaven.

Stand by me

Generally speaking, after the first six weeks you will most likely find that the Erstwhiles and the Thrushes will move off the map and you will no longer be on their radar. This can be for a variety of reasons. There is a spectrum here from wondering what to do and being unsure about how to respond at one end, to a calculated decision which goes, 'Well, she was really my friend; I didn't know him or the girls that well,' at the other. All of this I would call normal and understandable.

As a race the English are really not always adept at managing or expressing emotions and so quite often this kind of abdication of a friendship and its responsibilities can happen.

What really hurts though are the friends who your spouse loved, who while she was alive took all they could from her and gave a great deal to her as well, but once she's gone choose to evaporate.

To me and my daughters, that felt at the time like we'd all loved these people and invested in them, only to find out that we experienced another kind of bereavement when they vanished from our lives. And that made us grieve again in a whole new way.

When it comes to such people you try very hard not to be cynical but, as someone once said, 'I forgive. And I move on. But I don't go back to a dog that bites.'

A friend of mine once said to me, 'You can't be a mile wide and an inch deep.' I think he has a point. It takes an enormous amount of energy and work to maintain multiple layers of relationships and twelve years down the road I am still working things through in that regard.

A primal reaction

Anyway let's backtrack a little. Right now you're in the furnace and everything feels incredibly sensitive and raw. You feel lost and yet you must continue to live, to get up in the morning and have the courage to face the day and dare to live again. But how do you do that?

Don't ask me why, but there is something about a person dying that makes you want to go forth and multiply. This in fairness may not apply to those in the later years of life but for anybody from their twenties to fifties it is, in my experience, fairly typical. Maybe it's the finality of death that evokes this primordial urge, an urge that engulfs us like a giant tsunami, an urge in which we ache to create life. I don't know. But I do know it's a strange but natural reaction and that it can prove very complicated.

You see if you've been nursing your spouse for a long time, your own needs for intimacy are not met. I'm not just writing about the physical aspect of relationships here. I'm talking about all the tiny vignettes of conversation that would normally take place in a day, the looks between the two of you that don't need words. These can get eroded over time as an illness progresses. Serious illness can do that; it can rob you of your intimacy.

Losing a loved one launches you into a lonely process and we can make mistakes, sometimes for the best possible reasons.

Six months after the funeral, I was just about coping. Well, let's be honest here. The children had their main meal at school and then in the evening I used to 'cook' either pizza or pasta or make toasted sandwiches with cucumber, crisps and tomatoes on the side.

I'm no Gordon Ramsay, although, in fairness, my family would say that in recent years I have improved!

I did my best to keep up with the ironing and washing and grooming the girls' hair, but I did on one occasion find myself sitting on our doorstep, about to do the school run, cutting my eldest daughter's toenails which had grown way too long!

I was, and remain, committed to all my children and doing the best I can for them, but I was struggling. Loneliness had kicked in big time and I was slowly and inexorably grinding through grief.

In all of this, I couldn't help remembering that my late wife had also told me in no uncertain terms that I should marry again.

Now let's just hold that thought shall we? What kind of woman who knows she is dying has the love, grace and courage in her heart to have such a conversation with her husband? I'll tell you – an extraordinary and earth-shatteringly remarkable emotional giant. That is the kind of woman I was married to.

So what did I do? I went looking for love with my vision and judgement clouded by grief. As a result, I spent time with a lovely soul who was also broken, grieving over her own issues. The net result was more brokenness.

This is what happens. Be prepared to make mistakes, because you will. But also be kind to yourself and those you love in the process. It is a moment in time and will not last forever.

Be kind to yourself

If I can offer maybe a couple more words of advice it would be this. If at all possible, for the first year, maybe even two, after you have lost your partner, make a pact with yourself that you will not date anyone.

Share this with your friends and also try not to make any other major decisions like moving house or giving precious family items away. Do nothing in haste. You are going through the most excoriating and brutal time.

At the same time, be kind to yourself. It doesn't matter if you mess up – it's all part of the journey. And where possible, be kind to the rest of the family because they are all going through a highly charged and turbulent time too.

It was the late, great George Harrison who sang 'All Things Must Pass' – and they will.

I promise you that.

It is just for a season.

3

Black Dog Days

After a great loss, one of the hardest things to endure is not just the loneliness and the fact that the world is going about its business while you feel broken in two – that is tough enough – but the sheer sense of abandonment, which can sometimes feel totally overwhelming. This is even starker when a loved one has taken their own life, leaving you to carry on alone. In one sense I regard this kind of finality, whether calculated or spur of the moment, as a cocktail of abject selfishness and ultimate sickness. It is difficult not to judge. And yet we must not. I can only imagine the torment that person must have been experiencing. Some of us may have wanted to give up, perhaps many times. Have you ever felt, in spite of the support of your family and faith, that if you didn't wake up in the morning it would be a blessing, not just for you but maybe for everyone? I'm no clinician but when you get to that stage I'd say that you're not just overwhelmed with despair but drowning in effluent, barely able to keep your head above water.

Survival strategies

Past experience tells me a number of things about conquering the citadel of abandonment. First of all, choose rest. Get more sleep and at the same time actively pursue ways of relaxing that work for you.

Secondly, try to get some exercise. I am hardly what can be described as a fine physical specimen but even I benefited, after my wife's death, by walking two to three miles every day. It gave me time to process things, as well as lose a few excess pounds!

I used to walk along the banks of the River Chess every working day processing my grief. Sometimes I would shout and scream. Sometimes I would cry and pray. And as the seasons changed I began to see beauty again and to feel alive. I became very aware of God's creation all around me, from the three trout beneath the bridge to the dragonfly hovering by my right shoulder as I walked.

Thirdly, it is also very easy to overeat and drink too much. If, like me, you love great food and fine wine, then try not to overindulge. However, with everything else going on don't beat yourself up too much if you occasionally do. You are in what I call the 'dread zone', where nobody would choose to go or wants to be. You have no choice other than to go through the fire and hopefully come out the other side.

Fourthly, as I mentioned in the last chapter, true friends (the Stoics) can be a great source of support and they can also help you learn how to have fun again. If all else fails, including your relationship with God – which let's face it may well feel distant and tenuous – then take a long and rigorous look at your family and friends. On the darkest days when I didn't want to get up, I just had to for my children's sake. Eventually I realized I also had to carry on for my own sake as well, although that life lesson can take a little longer to download. But kids or no kids, life can still be beautiful. We just have to see it. And beginning to see again takes time after a trauma.

Two years after my wife died I walked into the lobby of a friend's home and remarked how lovely it was and how the colours they had chosen for the walls looked so fresh. They smiled.

'It's been that way for three years now,' they remarked.

I had been so bound up and lost in the pit of grief that I hadn't been able to see.

Fifthly, and this will sound like a terrible cliché, be kind to yourself.

Letting off steam

I had always had a reputation for not suffering fools gladly and to this day I suppose that is still the case. It's not something about which I am proud and throughout my wife's illness I tried to keep a lid on my anger. Those who knew me well understood just how ticked off I was by everything, but I did my best to plough on and put on a brave face.

In spite of my best efforts, however, my rage would come to the surface at odd moments: when I was behind the wheel of a car, for example (I know what you're thinking; 'he's a typical male'), or at a party when I would let my hair down a little too much (I have very little hair but please indulge the metaphor). Now and again when I was with my best friends it would boil over after a bottle of wine, and colourful words and invectives would accompany my tears.

So I had always been in need of a bit of anger management but after my wife passed, I didn't have to hide my anger quite so much. I remember one time when my youngest daughter, out of a mixture of anger and grief, had locked herself in the downstairs bathroom and was refusing to come out. I kicked the door in, pulled her out and hugged her. That was not exactly textbook stuff but you sometimes have little or no emotional resources left; we simply have to make it up as we go along.

On another particularly tough day I suggested that all three of us lie face down on the bed and scream into the mattress at the top of our lungs. We did and we all felt a lot better for it.

Music and films were also helpful. We would watch family movies together and sing our favourite hit songs in the car at the top of our lungs.

I can recall driving round the M25 having just been to see the Jack Black movie *School of Rock*, and we had the stereo on. We were singing our own version: 'Don't let go, you've got the music in you, one dance left, you know we're gonna pull through.' That became one of our family anthems. Moments like these helped us let off steam.

Please remember though, this is a process. It takes time to release the anger and it takes time for that anger to dissipate. I can still see the effects on myself and my daughters eleven years on and, yes, at times I am still sometimes angry. Why? Because what happened then can still affect us in the choices we make now – the good and the bad – and in how we live out our faith and lives.

However, it does get easier, less jagged – and letting off steam is all part of the healing.

Feeling abandoned

One of the most helpful things you can do is go to God when you feel abandoned.

Let's look at the feeling of being abandoned.

Are we right to feel bereft, lost and lonely? Most certainly.

Are we, or should we, even feel angry? Of course. It is a perfectly natural reaction.

Won't God be offended if we express our anger towards him when we feel this way? No. I really don't think so.

If we are in an authentic relationship with God, as opposed to simply ticking a religious box when we feel like it, then we have to say what we feel. We have to be able to come right out with it in our prayers. And here's the good news: when we do, Jesus understands. Think about it for a moment. There's nothing like hanging on a cross with your body broken and your lifeblood ebbing away to underscore that. God knows pain. He feels our pain, and he wants to help us through.

When Jesus was hanging on a Roman cross outside Jerusalem he shouted, 'My God, my God, why have you abandoned me?' (Mark 15:34 NLT.) He looked up to the heavens and shouted the equivalent of 'God, where are you?' This is an agonizing moment. For the first and the only time in his life, Jesus was not aware of the Father's affectionate presence and his loving embrace.

Jesus, as the Son of God, had a special relationship with his Father in heaven. At his baptism in the River Jordan, he saw the heavens open and heard his heavenly Father say, 'You are my beloved son and I'm really proud of you' (my paraphrase). Now, several years later, he's hanging on a cross, dying for the sins of the world. That sin – our sin – causes Jesus to feel that the heavens are now closed and that his Father is no longer there.

What an indescribable loss that must have been in Jesus' broken, human heart?

But here's the point.

When you feel as if your Father in heaven is far away, that he's abandoned you, and all you have is this inner rage against the dark clouds that surround you, you can take comfort in the fact that Jesus understands. He's been there. He has walked your walk, felt what you feel, entered the heart of darkness as you have.

Even though this may not answer the question why (why has this happened?), it will help you to know that Jesus is familiar with grief and that he knows what it is to be a Man of Sorrows. As the Book of Isaiah chapter 53 says, he is 'a man of suffering, familiar with pain' (NIV).

Taking your blues to God

All this may get you thinking about church and how that featured in my life after Lynn died, and how it might feature in your life if you're travelling down the gravel road of grief.

We were blessed that our church family had, and still has, a huge pastoral heart. People tolerated me when I scowled at them or was grumpy, which in fairness was (and can still be) quite often, but they somehow seemed to get the balance just right, so that they weren't tapping us on the shoulder all the time, asking us how we were, but were still there for us if we needed them – which we did, often.

I took my lead from Johnny Cash and dressed as the 'Man in Black' for six months. To be honest it felt right and it felt appropriate. I was letting the world and my church know I was hurting and they'd better watch out!

I was very, very angry with God. Why did he take my wife when there were other feckless, horrible people busy stuffing up his planet? How dare he leave my children without a mum! He was supposed to be in charge, wasn't he? Why had he let this happen?

Not surprisingly, in this state it was hard to worship God. But it was important for us as a family to be going to church at least to try. The church provided a place of grace and love where we were for the most part allowed just to be. However, on occasion some of the songs just didn't make sense. How could people be so bland and corporately blind? As far as I was concerned he wasn't the 'faithful one, so unchanging'. He was the 'unfair one', who had some serious explaining to do – not so much the 'air I breathe' as a toxic fog of gloom that I was thrashing around in.

It took time. I am a stubborn man. But then God is still God and he used the one medium I love to get to me – music.

It was no Damascus Road experience but over a period of twelve months I was asked to play in the worship band in church and it was through playing my heart out, taking my blues to God as an offering, that I came through and started to smile again.

Responding to abandonment

A Christian called David Watson once said this: 'There are no easy answers, only good responses.' When we are confronted by abandonment, there are practical responses and spiritual responses. On a practical note, I have suggested the following in this chapter:

- Choose rest
- Take exercise
- Don't overindulge
- Enjoy your friends
- Be kind to yourself (especially when you don't manage to achieve any of the above!)

On a spiritual note, try to connect with God. Where you relate best to God is where he will find you. It could be in sport, art, reading, walking or anything, but he will be there at the right time, gently extending a hand and patiently waiting.

The one thing that will get in the way of all this is our very human and insistent need to have an answer to the question, 'Why?'

This can often actually begin before your loved one dies. When you are caring for someone with a long-term illness you try to make a deal with God – 'Just let her see the girls grow up and I'll promise to be a better man,' or, 'Take me instead of her. Girls need their mum.' But God doesn't play this game. He knows all the days of our lives. He's the Potter and we are the clay. And pots don't get to dictate to the one who makes them! A scary thought, isn't it?

The trouble is, sometimes we are so desperate that we forget these things and become downright irrational. We will believe anything and do anything if we think God will make our loved one better.

I'll be honest here: if my wife had told me to stand on my head in the corner of a crowded restaurant stark-naked singing, 'Make Me a Channel of Your Peace', I swear I would have done it.

Maybe you won't be surprised, then, to hear that out of desperation we even resorted to using Traditional Chinese medicine. While the treatments arguably provided a placebo effect, they also caused the entire house to stink for days on end with the foetid, rank odour of dried bark. I'll never forget that smell and I have no intention of using it again.

However, that stench was much more easily endured than the letter written to us by one church member who felt the cancer might be as a result of sin in the past.

Whether we like it or not, conscious or otherwise, we can sometimes believe that there is a game to be played with God – like *Deal or No Deal*. However, our lives are not ours to negotiate.

So in my case, I came to the sad conclusion that bad stuff happens in life. It was just our turn. All of us will have to deal with loss at some point. That is, after all, why I'm writing this book. It's just that for some of us it comes earlier than we'd expect or want. I don't know why God did what he did, and I may never know until I get to the next life, but it is my fervent belief that it is better to live with faith than without it, even if the only reason you believe in God is because of the beauty of a mountain in the Peak District or the crashing of the waves on a Cornish shore. You may not be a card-carrying member of a church, but it is what it is.

So connect with God if you can.

And don't be religious. Be real.

When you're going through the raw agony of feeling abandoned, this is not the time for rhetoric. It's the time for raging. It's the time for the prayer of the heart. It's time for telling God about your sense of his absence, the feeling that he's abandoned you and your anger at all that's happened to you.

This is a time for raging against the dying of the light, to paraphrase the Welsh poet Dylan Thomas.

So my advice is this: let Jesus in when you can. He will be waiting. And that feeling of being left outside alone will pass.

We all have 'black dog days', as Winston Churchill used to call them.

Even Jesus did.

4

Learning to Live Again

Mother's Day came hard on the heels of my wife's passing and was a brutal and stark reminder of all that my little girls had lost. We somehow got through it, but I honestly can't remember how. We spent Easter with my dad and his wife in Cornwall. That was tough but bearable. Then it was Father's Day, when Lynn would have cooked me a full English breakfast and she and the children spoilt me rotten. I was truly blessed, and remain so, to have friends like David and Carrie who knew what a tender day it would be and who together with the girls had bought me a beautiful framed photograph of our daughters and a gorgeous shirt.

For my daughters' birthdays I have to admit I over-compensated, at one point even hiring a stretch limousine. Grief makes you do strange things. I guess I was just trying to create new memories.

We went down to visit my parents a lot and we continued to see Lynn's mum and dad. That was hard because they had invested so much in the children and their house was full of happy memories. Yet it was also so painful to be there because the one person we all loved was missing.

It took me a couple of years before I felt comfortable staying overnight, which must have hurt Lynn's parents, but the problem was I couldn't stand the pain. I wish now that I'd found the inner strength to grasp the nettle, but the truth was that I was deep in the valley and it would take time and courage to begin the long climb up and out. Bound up in my own journey, I wish I had found the grace to give more to others.

One year on

I remember our first Christmas as a family on our own. It was tough. I went over the top, with loads of presents for the girls. My best friend and his wife came round to our house with their children and we did Christmas together. Having a crowd around somehow made it more bearable, although when I look at the photographs taken that day we all look lost. But I thought at the time that if, on days like these, we kept busy and surrounded ourselves with friends and family then it somehow would be easier to survive. It was only when everybody left and I'd put the girls to sleep that I'd sit with my faithful dog Max on my lap and cry my heart out and wonder if I'd ever find true happiness again.

So the seasons came and went. A year had flown by and then one day it was 20 February – the day Lynn had died.

A bunch of her closest and most faithful friends joined the children and me in Oxford, where the church was opened especially for us. I put together a book of my favourite photographs and wrote underneath each one. I also carefully selected some music that reminded me of her: Johnny Mathis singing, 'A Certain Smile'.

And my heart was broken one more time as I, along with my friends and family, honoured her memory and continued to let her go, as we sat there bonded by sorrow, listening, crying and calling out to God.

The hardest year of my life was over.

Now what?

Making records again

It takes courage to move through the years after the loss of a loved one, but move we must. Life has to move on. It has to keep moving forward. It is what *they* would have wanted and it is also what we have to do.

We have to choose life.

Our loved ones would want us to.

Just after the first anniversary of my wife's death I was asked to go and talk to Decca Records about a job. I wasn't sure how I felt about going back into a working environment like the music business, or any kind of employment for that matter, but I needed to earn a living and think about some kind of future. For years, my life and career had felt like it had been in a holding pattern. I explained my predicament to the company – about my bereavement and about being a single parent – and I have to say for a corporation they were wonderful. A job was created where I would work three days a week as a consultant for them and the rest of the time I could work from home. This was a God-send. In addition, a good friend of the family agreed to pick up my daughters from school and to feed and look after them until I came home at 7 p.m.

All this, I felt, was God's grace working to great effect through other people at work and at home. It meant that I was able to start enjoying work again, making records with Russell Watson, Michael Ball and Engelbert Humperdinck, among others.

I had an assistant, and a lot of women worked in the office. Although I was shy at first, I grew in confidence. I developed a deep platonic friendship with one lady signed to the company, which I treasure to this day.

Life is not a dress rehearsal

This was a cathartic time. I had been unsure about the whole dating thing, having made one mistake already, but there was a sense in which I was being prepared to risk loss again, as Marlene Dietrich would say, by 'Falling in Love Again'.

And love is a risky business isn't it? There are no cast-iron guarantees, as the statistics for divorced couples clearly show. Having suffered great loss it made me even more determined to enjoy my life and all the time I have left – to celebrate every breath I get to take.

To glory in living the life God gave us.

Wring out every last heartbeat.

Why?

Because life can be short and then we die.

So enjoy.

Do not let life pass you by.

Climb that mountain.

Leap out of that plane.

Love unconditionally.
This is not a rehearsal.
Don't be a spectator.
You get one life.
So live it!

PART II
LIFE STORIES

Introduction

Rough Diamonds

Grief comes in all shapes and sizes and is as unique and individual as a rogue cell.

I have written about my own story of grief in the first part of this book but I also want to acknowledge that there are many other facets of grief. In a sense grief is like a rough diamond – a piece of rock that's mined and then slowly chipped away. It can be cut a myriad of different ways to reveal its flaws and facets.

Let's look at a few of the different forms of grief.

There is first of all grief over lost opportunities. Many women suffer this kind of grief. I believe there's a whole generation of women who bought the lie could that they can have it all – the glittering career, the handsome husband and the ideal 2.4 children, or whatever today's version is. They may well have battled through the maelstrom of a male-dominated business, overworked and by comparison been underpaid, to get somewhere like their male counterparts have. They have strained every sinew to seek purpose and fulfilment, while striving for parity and equality. They have watched their best friends from college get married and have children. These friends may have picked up the pieces after an ugly divorce, but at least they have children.

What these career women have by comparison is a comfortable lifestyle with plenty of holidays (don't forget to pack your smartphone) but their social life may well revolve around work. They're always first into the office, last to leave and then will be 'available' on their phone later should the boss call to discuss something.

It is possible that women like this may have come close to getting married a couple of times and may have had their heart broken too, but they now mourn the hourglass figure they once possessed and remember that their body clock is ticking. Pretty soon they will no longer be able to enjoy that most precious and finite of journeys – pregnancy and then birth. I know lots of women like this and my heart breaks for them. Even as a man, I know that after my wife died I'd look at another couple and envy their closeness and the way they positively oozed vitality and health. On occasions I'd think, 'How come we got the short straw?'

I believe there are perhaps many women and, yes, men too, who grieve over the lack of a permanent committed relationship and a family.

Then there is a second kind of grief – this time tied up with work and identity. Very often the first thing men will say to each other after the initial introduction is, 'What do you do?' It is as if our self-worth is inextricably linked and bound to our job.

Here is a short (we'll call it) fictional story.

Jack Wetherall had worked in the steelworks in Sheffield all his life, as had his father before him, and his granddad too. In those days the city was synonymous with the steel industry.

If you checked your mum and dad's cutlery drawer back in the 1960s, each knife, fork and spoon would bear the legend 'Sheffield Steel'. Viners was one of the best-known local firms and steel dominated the city and its workforce. Rabone Chesterman made steel rulers. BSC made huge girders. The evidence was everywhere.

Then in the 1980s there came a new kind of politics and people in the North of England took a clattering, especially the miners and the steelworkers. Thousands were made redundant.

The steel mill in Tinsley was one of the first to go and three generations of Wetheralls' work was destroyed overnight with the swift, autocratic movement of one signature. Jack had been at the steelworks for 30 years and had a pension of sorts, but it was barely enough to put food on the table for him and his wife, let alone pay for visits down to London to see his son and family. A proud man, he could no longer afford to buy his round at the working men's club in Tinsley on Saturday nights. So he stopped going. His wife Margery did a bit of cleaning for the richer folk who lived on the other side of the city, but by the time she'd paid her bus fares there and back there wasn't exactly a lot to take home.

One Saturday afternoon, while Jack was watching the wrestling on the television, as his favourite tag team the Royal Brothers were about to enter the ring, the bailiffs knocked on his door. They walked in, ripped the plug out of the wall, and repossessed the telly. With that went Jack's last escape.

That night Jack calmly broke into his neighbour's house, nicked his car keys from off the mantel and drove up onto the ridge called Ringinglow. There, high above the city, looking down at the gleaming lights and dead industry, he shoved a hose over the exhaust, switched the ignition on and drank the best part of a bottle of whisky before passing into a toxic sleep from which he was never to awaken.

You see, men need to work and, although men's identities need to be found in God, most often when blokes meet each other the first question they ask is, 'What do you do?' So when we lose a job or we get too old for the industry we're in, it hurts. We can get depressed, grumpy, drink too much, put on weight, maybe even have affairs. Why? We are lost. When we worked and could provide for our families we felt good. There may have been a hefty mortgage but we'd cover it. We might even have had two cars parked in the driveway and holidays abroad every year. Life was good.

Wasn't it?

Maybe, but was it all in perspective?

Is there such a thing as a job for life? Not in Jack Wetherall's case, sadly. It does not really exist these days. But there are lots of us in the same boat, and it needn't be called the Titanic. So, if from time to time you get that sinking feeling, don't be like Jack – talk to someone. Share the grief. Don't hide your heart and hurt away.

Then there's a third kind of grief – the grief of divorce. When vows are broken and you find out that the person you promised to spend the rest of your life with is not all they appeared to be, when the sacred promises that were made are broken and you are left with a relationship lacking any substance, then mistrust rears its ugly head, alongside those awkward bedfellows doubt and deceit. That is indeed one of the loneliest places on God's earth and, once again, it is an experience of loss. When we lose the ability to trust, then we have lost everything.

If a partner is unfaithful, how can you ever trust them again? Will you spend too much time wondering if they'll just carry on indulging themselves, except perhaps more discretely?

Should we forgive in these situations? Well, I think the answer has to be yes. That's very easy to write but tough to actually do and keep doing. I have known a lot of couples in this position, some Christians, some not. Sometimes people, regardless of faith or position, *do* get divorced. But it is not just the husband and wife who lose; where there are children involved, they too sip from the bitter cup. Nowadays, there are as many 'blended' families as traditional ones but loss is the great common denominator.

How can the pain of divorce be turned around? The truth is, I don't know. I'm not sure it can. If people can find true love in a new relationship, one that has integrity and keeps its vows sacred, then maybe there is a security in that for all the family.

So divorce is fundamentally loss. But this loss starts when we don't pay attention to our partner, when we don't listen, when we fail to compromise, when we put our needs ahead of theirs and fail to check in with God.

Our thought life can also be very unhelpful. As a man, I can look at a woman and think, 'you are b-e-a-u-t-i-f-u-l', but if then I look again and imagine her naked or take a sneaky look at her breasts then I've crossed the line and I'm now in a minefield. So we must actively take measures to protect ourselves and those we love, and in the process we can help ourselves.

If I am really honest, I rarely put myself under the microscope and examine what makes me tick. However, if I did, I think on occasions it would reveal a man who, despite his best efforts, is rather selfish, has an internal dialogue which is far from helpful, would like to be waited on 24/7 in an ideal world, and could have a much better relationship with his Lord and Creator. All of this can seriously hinder a marriage.

For those who end up divorced, it can be a lonely road and the church and its people are not always as understanding as they should be or even might like to be. It is, after all, easy to judge, but then the verse that springs to mind is, 'There is now no condemnation for those who are in Christ Jesus (Romans 8:1)'. I know even as I write that people will be saying, 'Ah, well, but if they'd been in Christ in the first place none of this would have happened!' If only life was that easy. Well, to you I say, 'Let he who is without sin cast the first stone' (see John 8:7), and try not to throw it in my direction. I bruise easily.

So there are many different kinds of grief, but what they all have in common is that they leave people feeling guilty.

When a loved one dies this is especially true. We can be full of questions and thoughts such as:

'If only I hadn't lived so far away.'
'If only I'd listened more.'
'I should have given more time.'
'I should have been less selfish.'
'If I'd been there that morning it would all have been all right.'

'I wish I'd known him/her better.'

'If only he'd asked I'd have helped out.'

'Why didn't he/she tell me how ill they really were last time I came?'

'I didn't know he/she suffered from depression' . . .

While it is normal to ask questions when someone dies, and a certain amount of self-examination can be helpful, I don't believe we're called to don a hair shirt and metaphorically beat ourselves with a big stick. Frankly that is not acceptable. As I've written in Part I, we need to be kind to ourselves. We don't just need to forgive others, we need to forgive ourselves.

And we need to keep a sense of perspective. This life isn't all there is. Death doesn't have the last word. Grief is not the end of the story.

For the Christian this should be the case. We're headed for eternity. What is there really to fear, besides the process by which we get there? We must keep in mind our eternal destination as we live through the ups and downs of life. That is not to belittle any of the stages of loss and loneliness. Rather it is to try to place it gently in a right perspective.

In Part II we will look at people who have experienced different facets of the rough diamond of grief and who at the same time managed to put that grief into some kind of eternal perspective.

Throughout my own journey I have been blessed to meet other fellow travellers on the gravel road of love, loss and loneliness. They have a common denominator in that they are all prepared to share their treasures of darkness and be vulnerable.

In some cases, where I have been asked, I have changed their names. In every case their stories are both humbling and inspiring.

My prayer is that they encourage and envision you to turn the rough diamond of your own grief into a dazzling gem of hope.

5

Peter and Rachel

I first met Peter and Rachel at the Greenbelt Arts Festival in England back in 2009. We were taking part in a bereavement seminar hosted by Jonathan Mayo and were on a panel of so-called experts, along with the lovely Sister Frances from Helen House in Oxford. Rachel had given birth to four children but two of them had very sadly died from a rare illness known as Batten's disease. I found her and Peter's faith and love humbling and inspiring.

Fragile yet faith-filled, Peter and Rachel have created a home that's calm and serene, filled with photographs taken by Pete which beautifully capture this remarkable family.

They, along with so many others, are unsung heroes and broken warriors from the gravel road of grief.

This is their story:

Peter and Rachel were married twenty-four years ago, though looking at them now they hardly look old enough. Rachel is a nurse and Pete has a photographic business. As a couple they decided to enjoy time together before having kids, so it wasn't until six years into married life that their first daughter, Misha, was born. She was due on Christmas Day 1995 but actually arrived early, on 14 November. Rachel had high blood pressure and so the birth was induced. It was a difficult and complicated birth, and two hours afterwards Rachel coughed and lost a massive amount of blood, causing her to pass out. Chaos ensued, with an emergency medical team rushing in.

Pete: 'It was very scary. This was our first child and dads like me don't really know what's what. But clearly, having the room full of medics and people made me realize that this wasn't very normal.'

Rachel was rushed to the operating theatre and Pete was told not to worry, that everything would be fine and that she'd be back soon.

After the longest five hours of his life, waiting outside the operating theatre and the Special Care Baby Unit, Pete was allowed to see Rachel. When he did he found her 'fitting' on the bed. It turned out her body was allergic to the anti-sickness drug she'd been given post-surgery.

Rachel: 'I had one of those last-minute, dark-tunnel moments with the light at the end. I was looking back, seeing Pete holding Misha, and saying, "I'm not ready".'

Rachel had nearly died. Her face and hands were swollen following the trauma, but after a while this calmed down. Misha was a little jaundiced from the birth but, apart from that, was doing well. Having spent two weeks in the special baby care unit, the three of them were finally united at home.

Six months later Rachel went back to work as a nurse. She was on duty three nights a week. This proved to be a very challenging time for them as a couple, culminating in them nearly splitting up.

Pete had felt marginalized by the new arrival, plus Rachel had been suffering from post-natal depression so, as he puts it, 'I felt pushed away and, very unfairly, searched for love and comfort in the arms of somebody else. This brought its own tensions and by the Christmas of 1996 I was living in a squat in Buckingham. There I stayed for three or four months. These were tough times, but ones that made me realize what a stupid boy I'd been. I thank God that Rach took me back in the new year of 1997.'

Peter and Rachel somehow managed to fall in love all over again and had a second honeymoon. As you might expect, it took a lot of work; the issue of trust was a massive mountain for them to climb. But they made it and, as Christmas of that year beckoned, they went out for a meal with friends to celebrate life and the impending arrival of their second child. But half way to the restaurant in Wendover, Rachel said to Pete, 'I think you'd better take me to the hospital.' Forty-five minutes later she gave birth to Natalie. Two-year-old Misha now had a precious baby sister.

However, work for Pete was thin on the ground and he had to take a job as a shop fitter in Aberdeen for three or four months. Once again this was a really tough time with money scarce and Rachel at home with two small children.

Soon after, Pete retrained as a photographer and subsequently got some work experience in London with Amanda Burton's husband, Sven Arnstein. He worked on shoots for *Hello!* and the *Radio Times* featuring a number of celebrities, from *Men Behaving Badly* star Neil Morrissey to the former *Generation Game* co-host Anthea Redfern.

In May of 1999 Pete and Rachel went down to Port Isaac with some friends. It had been a long journey down to Cornwall and they'd just arrived and unpacked. The sun was shining and the sea was shimmering. It was a perfect day.

Misha and Natalie were running around and laughing when all of a sudden they went quiet.

Pete: 'Misha stood in front of us. She stopped motionless. Her eyes were flickering and she looked like she was having a seizure.'

Rachel: 'I thought it would go straight off, but it carried on.'

Her mother's instinct, along with her nursing training, kicked in and Rachel scooped Misha up in her arms, carried her into the front room and gave her a hug.

Misha had by now turned blue.

Rachel very quickly unblocked Misha's airway. She then put her in the recovery position. Their friends phoned the ambulance and Pete and Rachel prayed for their little girl as they waited for it to arrive. Thankfully 3-year-old Misha came out of the fit and was taken to Truro hospital, falling asleep on the way there. The hospital ran a series of tests and the next morning she woke up, ran around the ward and everything appeared to be back to normal.

Pete: 'We'd phoned all the family at this point and I remember standing outside Truro hospital saying, 'Please pray!'

The doctor's findings indicated an epileptic seizure or febrile fit and they were told not to worry unduly but follow it up with their doctor when they got back home.

Just four short weeks later Misha had another episode.

Rachel: 'All I remember is her starting to fall downstairs and not being able to stand properly.'

The seizures became more frequent until they were coming every two to three weeks. Misha would enter almost a coma-like state. Peter and Rachel were given various drugs to try and help her, but they didn't really make much difference. Misha had just been potty-trained. Then her speech started to go, so she had grommets fitted.

Rachel: 'She never really developed her speech.'

Pete: 'We started getting called in for ECGs, ERGs (electro-retinograms) – all sorts of stuff.'

They were referred to the John Radcliffe hospital in Oxford as Christmas of 1999 approached. The whole world was gearing up for the new millennium and Misha had just turned 4 years old. Rachel was pregnant with their third child, Sophie. Natalie at this point was a bundle of fun and mischief, often making her parents smile with her tomboy antics.

On Christmas Eve, Peter and Rachel were called into the John Radcliffe and told by the consultants that they'd like to do a skin biopsy on Misha. With her nursing background Rachel knew they were looking for something very specific. She asked the doctor what they were looking for and it was at this point that they first heard the term Batten's Disease.

Pete: 'The doctors said they were looking for Batten's Disease and that they wanted to rule it out, as it is horrible. At this time, most of the world had yet to go on the Internet so we asked our dear friends David and Theresa to look up Batten's disease for us. I still remember the day Theresa came to the door.'

Rachel: 'She said the description matched Misha's age, her fitting, her inability to stand and her falling, as well as her speech – all of that stuff. We talked about blindness and then death. So we knew what we were looking at.'

They waited four weeks before getting the test results.

Pete: 'I think when we read the thing we knew it fitted Misha to a tee, and we just cried in each other's arms at that moment, really. From that point on I guess we were numb. Although we were waiting on the tests we threw a massive millennial party, put a great big tarpaulin up over our and our neighbour's gardens, put straw matting down, invited every family member and neighbour that we could and had a wild party. We got quite drunk and threw ourselves into a bit of oblivion really. We didn't mind too much if we didn't wake up, but at that point Rachel was pregnant so we had to be careful.'

Pete's voice tails off and then he quietly says, 'We were at the hospital on 30 January 2000. Sophie had just been born, and then literally within minutes we got a phone call from the John Radcliffe hospital saying, "Oh, we've got your test results." So we said, "No thanks!"'

Rachel laughs. 'I'd just given birth and said, "Can we leave it a week?"'

Pete: 'We were just putting off the inevitable news of what Misha had. I remember Dr Pike, our consultant, calling us over a week later and the giveaway was the Batten's Disease Family Association leaflets on the table, placed beside a box of tissues. Obviously we knew. But he was great; he said, 'I've got as long as you need.' It was the end of the day, about five o'clock. 'I'm here for you and I'll answer any questions you've got,' he said. He was truly a man of God, whether he knew it or not – a gentleman who was being Jesus to us in that moment of desperation, *sheer* desperation.'

What Peter and Rachel didn't realize for a while was that this is a genetic disease, which meant that they both had to pass on the recessive gene. In effect, any child they have together has a one in four chance of displaying it, and a one in two chance of carrying it.

Rachel: 'Having three children by that point . . .'

At this point Rachel's voice tailed off and I glimpsed a tiny fragment of their grief. But I could also see a brave and valiant couple, who loved God and continue to do so.

A little while later they went on to lose both Misha and Natalie to Batten's Disease.

It is not the normal order of life for a child to die before a parent. It's just not right. Nor is it fair to see not one but two of your children die in such a long and painful way.

It is not for me to try to describe this grief because it would be an injustice to Misha and Natalie and to their parents. Mere words are inadequate here.

Somehow Peter and Rachel have survived loving, losing and the desolate loneliness that comes with all of that.

Life has not crushed them and by the grace of God they have found the strength with him to endure, and they have two more children who do not suffer from the disease.

6

Precious Cargo

Gaye is a glamorous lady in her mid-fifties. She's a bit of an intellectual. A journalist by trade, she believes in God but the road she has walked has at times been far from easy.

Over the course of an hour, as she recounted her tale, I was moved by her bravery and her commitment to her faith. She freely admits that, even though it's a cliché, God is her rock. She has suffered great loss but has also come to a place of peace.

As a young woman Gaye was not brought up in a Christian household but says that she had an awareness of God right from the start. She remembers a vicar coming to her school. She also recalls how the story of the nativity, and even nature itself, made a deep impression on her. She has always had that sense of 'something else'. 'I think it was God,' she says.

At the age of 15 she was confirmed and wore a little white dress and a matching veil. It was 'quite a celebration'. She had expected something amazing to happen, but it did not. It wasn't until 11 years later that she realized that nobody had ever talked to her about asking Jesus into her life, or if they had, she hadn't heard it.

The church she went to was quite lively, with lots of young people, but it was also a traditional village church. So for a long time the freedom of a real relationship with God was missing.

Gaye consequently started to drift away from God. She moved house and then holidayed in Italy where she met a man who would later become her husband. When she returned, she began her time at Oxford University where she studied French and German.

All this happened in the 'swinging sixties', the era of Mary Quant, the Beatles, Twiggy, psychedelia and movies like *Alfie* and *The Italian Job*.

Aware of that wonderful spirit of optimism that hung in the air – the feeling that anybody could do anything – Gaye was keen not just to complete her academic studies but to taste all that life had to offer. Infused with idealism, by her own admission, she thought she could change the world, so she went on marches to the American Embassy in Grosvenor Square in London to protest against the Vietnam War. In her first week at university she joined the Anarchists' Society. As she recounts this part of the tale we both laugh at the delicious irony of it all. You'd have to travel a long way to meet someone less anarchistic than Gaye.

All this was, of course, a contradiction in terms. How can a group of anarchists have a society? The real reason she joined was because she hoped to gain access to a regular supply of marijuana – which she smoked regularly, though not to the detriment of keeping up with her studies.

Gaye's Italian boyfriend turned up for the summer vacation. However, Gaye wasn't feeling great about the relationship as the holiday drew to a close. He could be manipulative on occasions and quite 'out of it' (for whatever reason!) for the majority of the time. Gaye's assessment was that he didn't seem to spend much time in the 'real world'.

Gaye went back to Oxford for the new term and then discovered she had an ectopic pregnancy. 'I nearly died. It completely messed me up. It was awful, absolutely awful.' She told the doctors at the John Radcliffe hospital not to tell her parents but in the end she couldn't keep it a secret. 'I was just all over the place; it was horrendous.'

Gaye told her parents that she didn't want to go back to Oxford and then rang her boyfriend in Italy. In the process they somehow talked themselves into getting married.

'I thought getting married would sort everything out.'

Gaye had experienced the loss of a child, the trauma of telling her parents and then abandoning her course at university. All that potential – was it gone?

'There's something very instinctive, especially in women. Your hormones are all up the creek. Yet even though I'd gone off the rails and been a bit wild, I wasn't promiscuous. My weight, however, dropped to 7 stone and my father was desperately upset. Something inside me wanted things to be right because basically I'm a 'proper' person. Even before I became a Christian I was brought up 'properly' and had a very happy childhood and lovely parents. I just rebelled, basically – nothing unusual. I thought by getting married everything would be right.'

Gaye married the Italian in the town hall in Rome surrounded by his family. 'I don't want to do this, but I've got to do this because I'm here.' That's what she remembers feeling.

Gaye's parents did not attend but sent her a telegram to wish her well. Afterwards she became more and more unhappy and homesick.

'I remember seeing this parked MG Roadster with GB plates on it and thinking, maybe I can wait here until the owners come back and then I can ask them to take me home. I was so very unhappy. I knew I'd made a mistake but then discovered I was pregnant *again* almost immediately.'

Gaye told her husband she was going to pop home for a visit but didn't tell him she was carrying their baby. She packed everything and returned home to her mum and dad and told them the news. Their response was to try to get Gaye to reconcile with her Latin lover so that all would be as she puts it, 'proper'.

This is a word that regularly peppers her conversation and I wonder just how potent the effect of those six letters have been in her life, and just what expectations were placed on the little girl growing up. She was the jewel in the crown of her parents' relationship – shining, bright and gleaming. She didn't have a brother or sister to play with. She was an only child. Whatever her parents' expectations may have been, she was sure about one thing. She did not want to reconcile with the Italian. She couldn't bear to have the man near her. She was just 21.

Gaye's mum and dad were fantastic with her, and before long her son Ben was born. This should have been the cause of happiness, but it left her full of grief; she felt that she'd not only let herself down, but also her parents *and* her son because he didn't have a dad.

Gaye decided that her son ought to be christened, so after about a year she went along to her local church and shortly afterwards the vicar came round to see Gaye, her son Ben and her parents.

'He was terribly nice and we talked about spiritual things as well as where I was at. The thing I remember most was him talking about having a commitment to God, which struck home.'

They had a quiet, private service and Ben was christened.

Four years later, after much wrangling and dealing with the Italian legal system – which is literally a law unto itself, and felt like it at times – Gaye's divorce came through.

At the same time, she was invited by a couple from the church to an event to 'discuss the relevance of the Christian faith today'. The year was 1974.

'I looked at this invitation and thought, who are these people? I've never heard of them. Why have they sent this to me? So I rang the lady up and asked why she had invited me. 'I don't know you or anything,' I said.

The lady at the other end of the line patiently explained that the invitation was from her local church and the church was doing a mission under the banner, 'Faith in Focus'. Gaye had been invited because her son had been christened and people at the church had been praying for her and her family. Although Gaye was not feeling good about herself at the time, and her nerves were shredded (so much so that every time the phone rang she would leap in the air like a scalded cat), she decided to go along.

'I didn't know anybody. The host and hostess looked a bit nervous. We did the social bit and then we all sat down and listened to a little pep talk. After that a lady gave her testimony, at the end of which the bloke leading the evening asked, "Does anyone have any questions or comments?"

'There was silence.

'Then a young man said, "Well I think this is a load of rubbish!"

'As soon as he said that I knew which side I was on. I *knew*.

'The next Sunday I went to church and the vicar greeted me. I saw all these people worshipping God using the ancient 1662 prayers. I thought, "I want that. It's such a cliché, but I want that. Whatever they've got I want it." They were singing away and they all looked happy. I wanted that.

'I remembered, two years previously, this bloke called Barry outside a shop at Christmastime holding a carol service, pointing at the shop and shouting, "That's not what it's all about! This is what it's all about!" I was so embarrassed I cringed. I actually crossed the road. And yet here I was *in church*. The next Sunday I went back again and the talk was all about, "I have come that you might have life and have it in abundance." It was as if Jesus was calling me – just calling *me*.

'I always say it was like running down a slope and seeing a fruit machine with all the oranges coming up.

'Jackpot!

'That was it.

'The person at the front of the church gave this altar call, and here's another cliché for you – it was like somebody propelled me out of my seat and I couldn't stop myself. I was the first one there, down on my knees and that was the start of it.'

Gaye joined a home-group largely made up of people in their twenties and thirties, vibrant and colourful. They went through The Acts of the Apostles together, reading and studying it.

Gaye and Ben lived in a studio at the side of her parent's house. She started reading her Bible again and all the stuff she'd learnt as a child came flooding back to her. But one day, as she was reading, she felt that there was a nasty presence in the room which spooked her. 'It felt like the devil sitting there and laughing at me.' So Barry and John came down from the church to pray and cleanse the house.

'Barry took hold of my hands and invited the Holy Spirit to come but seemingly nothing happened.'

A couple of days later she was lying in a steaming hot bath late at night, hair in rollers, her face covered in face cream and she started thinking about Jesus. Suddenly she felt the urge to get out and kneel down.

'So I did. I wrapped a towel round me and knelt on the bath mat, put my hands out and started off by thanking Jesus for what he had done for me.

'And I was completely filled with the Holy Spirit.

'It started in my toes and went right up my body. Then it poured out of my mouth and I started speaking in tongues. I had no idea what I was doing but it felt wonderful. That was when my new relationship with God was sealed. And it was just so typical of God's sense of humour.'

Fast forward a few years and Gaye's life was getting back on track. She started to get to know a young man at her church who was hoping to become ordained. They began seeing each other and were getting along well. Then he was warned off her because she was divorced. Gaye was subsequently called to the church and told that she must not see him any longer; the relationship could never go anywhere as they would never be allowed to marry.

I would sincerely like to think that the church has grown up a little these days, but back then, that is how it was.

This was devastating for a young Christian lady who was on fire for the Lord and whose little boy didn't have a father.

'I felt like a second-class citizen and that it was deeply unfair. I cannot believe that God only *partially* redeems you. I didn't question God but I was very angry and didn't talk about what was going on to many people.'

It seems that nobody thought to sit down with Gaye and pray for the right man to come along and be her husband and to be a father to her son Ben.

At this point it is still possible to hear the pain and anguish that this conversation caused, though Gaye to her credit has, over time, learnt to forgive, and amazingly she has remained at the same church to this day.

I asked her, 'Where was God in all of this?'

'Well, God was still there because he was so real to me and I just couldn't deny that. I didn't turn away. I just knew he loved me. I was hurt, desperately hurt, but I didn't ever think it was God who caused me the pain. I thought it was people in his church and I was very sorry because I loved the Church of England. I felt hurt by this body that I'd joined which celebrated the fact that I had been redeemed one moment and then behaved as if I hadn't the next.'

I asked Gaye where she thought God was in the process of forgiving.

'Five months later I was helping at a house party and heard that this chap had become engaged. So that was the first step of healing. It immediately said to me, well, we were not meant for each other.

'I just carried on and the pain didn't come out for a long time, I think, because I then had the most horrific few years. My mother suddenly died. My father was still around, but we were all shell-shocked. It was absolutely awful because it was so sudden and she was only 56. My parents were completely devoted to each other.

'To cut a very long story short, even though Dad was devastated, not long afterwards he got engaged to somebody he'd met in Africa less than a year later.

'Ben and I flew out to Zimbabwe and met this lady. We knew immediately that she was the wrong person for my father. I couldn't say anything because I didn't have that sort of relationship with my dad. Nowadays, with this generation, I think it would be different.

'Beforehand I had prayed and prayed and prayed that I'd be able to welcome this person into the family. I always knew my dad would get remarried. I didn't have a problem with that because I have observed that people in successful marriages, when their partner dies (the men especially) usually get married again. But I thought he would get married to somebody who would give themselves to us and be as loving as I would have been if I was in that situation.

'It was also apparent that my dad didn't appear happy, but we were being taken round on this whistle-stop tour of Africa. We ended up at the Victoria Falls in this magnificent colonial hotel.

'Their relationship ended there.

'It was just like being in a book. While I was sitting drinking whisky with my dad late at night in this hotel lounge, he realized, from having Ben and me out there with this lady, that it wasn't going to work.'

So Gaye's father came back to England and was deeply unhappy. Then, just over a year later, he announced he was getting married again, and not only that, but his fiancée was pregnant. She was just three years older than his daughter.

Gaye says, 'Now I have a wonderful half-brother who is 25 and that's great. I've invested an awful lot of time and effort with him over the years and that's all good. But at the time my own son was just 12 years old. By all accounts he adored his granddad but, just when he needed a male role model, my father upped and left.'

Gaye was left to sort out the family home and all her late mother's belongings, which had never been dealt with. In effect, her father abdicated responsibility and left his daughter and grandson to clear up the emotional detritus that was left behind.

Not surprisingly, they felt bereft and abandoned.

Gaye continues, 'I think he went through a spell of madness. Grief comes out in different ways.'

So where was God in the midst of all this loneliness, anger and grief?

'I can only say he kept me going. I know that when Mummy died I was given a very clear sense that she'd gone into another room, and I hadn't realized I was frightened of dying. But she'd gone into the next room and it was as if she was saying, 'It's alright, I'm here.' You can call that whimsical or you can call that something that God has done for me. But it helped.

'Where I do say, "Why Lord?" and still do, is when I ask, "Why did you let my little boy grow up without a dad? Why didn't you provide him with a father?"

'I saw my son's face change overnight when my father left. Not only did Grandpa leave but there was a new baby boy on the scene (Dad's son) and a very prickly step-grandmother.

'It is my faith that has kept me going. If I hadn't had Jesus I suppose I would have become very depressed. I have been depressed but never chronically. I did think at one point of hanging myself from a door. That's how low I was. But it wasn't chronic depression. I don't get that kind of feeling any more.'

So now where is Gaye on her painful journey of love, loss and loneliness?

'Well, I've come to the point where I want to be more dependent on God. I've tried to work things out. I made those mistakes when I was very young, I made bad choices. That doesn't half shake your confidence; it makes you very nervous. So I've tended to look for security and be risk-averse. And I know I've been over-protective towards my son, which is probably the worst mistake I've made with him. I've done lots of good things but I'm now seeking the Lord and want to let go more. I don't feel my life is finished at all but I don't know what to do next.'

Gaye's walk has been hard. You could say that one event, when she was a hippy chick in the 1960s, shaped her life and yet God has redeemed that. I asked her, 'How do you see God's redemption working out and what more would you like to see him do?'

'The main thing I'd like to see him do is heal my son in every department but especially emotionally and spiritually. For me,

I don't know. I just take each day as it comes. One thing I do cling on to, though, is the fact that when you're redeemed, you're redeemed. You can't be half-redeemed. Either you are or you are not. And that is what gives my life meaning.

'I just know God's love. I just *know* it. Especially over the last couple of years.

'There was one time he sent me an angel. This was extraordinary. It was about three to four years ago. I was going off on my annual trip to South Africa to see my dad. I was at Heathrow and they called us onto the plane. I was walking down the gangway to board and wasn't really thinking about anything except looking forward to the flight. You know where the kink in the gangway is just before the plane? There was an angel there. I didn't actually see him. I knew he was there. He'd been waiting for me. He walked with me and it was so real as I boarded the plane I thought they (the cabin staff) were going to say something. I sat down in my seat and could feel the angel behind me.'

At this point I *had* to ask, 'How could you feel it?'

'It was just like a presence. I knew it was an angel. You couldn't see it, but it was so totally real. I don't know how to explain it. It was like being in the dark and there's somebody beside you. I knew it was there.

'So I sat in my seat. I was actually quite frightened but not fearful, so I sat there and said, "What's this with the angel, Lord?" and the words came back, "precious cargo". So I immediately thought, "Oh, there's somebody special on this plane. Maybe we're carrying one of those organs – a beating heart."

'You see, I always pray when I'm on a plane. I actually quite enjoy flying and I always pray that God will send his angels to bear us up and bring us safely down again.

'Then God said, "No, *you* are the precious cargo."

'I was overcome by that. It was just so wonderful.'

After all Gaye has been through, that is perhaps the best place to stop her story.

She has endured a great deal and experienced a lot of turbulence.

But she's also come to realize on the way that she's God's 'precious cargo'.

What a glorious gift.

7

Shakin' All Over

Barnaby Bloom is known as Barney to his friends and is 71 years old. He has been a Christian since 1972 and happily married for 37 years. He has two children – a son and a daughter both in their thirties. He has bright blue eyes that sparkle and dance mischievously as he talks. He is erudite, funny and one of life's great affirmers.

Barney was diagnosed with Parkinson's twenty-one years ago when he was just 50.

'The doc had thought it was just a benign tremor until my third visit when the neurologist said, "You've probably worked out that you have Parkinson's disease."'

When Barney first found out he was in a state of shock, so numb in fact that he had a car accident immediately afterwards, as he tried to leave the hospital.

'It was a flash car, one of these cars that would have cost thirty-thousand quid. The driver was absolutely furious. We exchanged numbers, but then I heard nothing from him. I guess his car was either stolen or not insured.'

I asked Barney how he felt when he heard the diagnosis.

'The first month, I thought death was imminent and I started clearing out the loft and getting my affairs in order.

I went to my GP who said I could have years to live, but I can't remember much more than that. We didn't tell the kids because our daughter was coming up to her GCSEs. We did tell some couples so that we could be prayed for, but we didn't really know what to expect.

'I had, some years previous to that, said to God that if ever I got anything nasty like cancer, that I would be a blessing in it and that I would shine for him.

'I became worried that I wouldn't be able to play with the kids like a normal dad would, and I was pretty pessimistic that I wasn't going to last too long.

'I felt sorry for my wife, that she was lumbered with someone who was so ill at such an early stage in life. She was wonderfully calm because she knew that stress is not good for Parkinson's and the slightest anxiety increases the symptoms. I was advised to give up work so that my "shelf life" would be longer.'

Barney gave up his job and his wife took on the role of the breadwinner as he became the man about the house. From then on the family had to put up with very rudimentary meals such as cabbage and potatoes and baked beans.

'It was hard for my wife to give away her influence in the kitchen but she was very good about that. She was amazing.'

He goes on. 'The symptoms were quite mild at first. My Bible study group and I used to watch my hands as I laid them on the table and the veins would start to "pop up" on the back of my hands. I thought that was funny.

'Over the years of living with the disease I relate myself a bit to the Apostle Paul who had to put up with ill health from time to time and yet God used him. We've entrusted ourselves to God and we believe that God is using us.'

I've known Barney for a few years now and seen him struggle with the effects of this disease, always with courage and a wonderful sense of humour.

Barney: 'The symptoms are shaking hands. I couldn't type like you are now. I have turn-off times in the day when suddenly I can't do things. For example, doing shirt buttons up can prove difficult. I have to be helped to dress sometimes. There are lots of little things. I get very tired. It can be very difficult with my posture. I tend to stoop. It also affects my waterworks so I'm wary of going anywhere. I can't walk as much as I used to. I stagger about. My facial expression freezes up and I can't smile as much as I used to, which is a drag because I like to smile but my face refuses to – which can come across as appearing stern, or that I disapprove of something. My speech isn't as good as it used to be. My wife would probably tell you other things as well.'

He recounts this list in a matter-of-fact way, but his tone is gentle and I feel tears rising in my eyes at his quiet humility and grace.

'I never get bitter. I might get "depressed", although one has to be very careful with this word. I get a bit down sometimes but I have too many blessings around me to get bitter. God's given me too much.

'I often think of the Kris Kristofferson song, "Why me Lord?" What did I ever do to deserve even one of these blessings I've known?

'I guess you could say that I have an attitude of gratitude. I try to make every day count and be aware of God's blessings to me and us and try to be an imparter of God's blessings to others. I try to keep a blessings diary.'

I ask Barney how he thinks he's survived so well for so long, and he says, 'I would put my long-term survival down to the presence of God in our lives. I don't honestly know. In the absence of knowing I put it down to my relationship with God my Father and the prayers of the saints. One just has to go ahead, go on and trust in God and say he's having his way, doing his thing.

'The marriage vows have been and remain very important, especially "In sickness and in health". My wife has supported me amazingly. I can't stress that too much. As a result of her support I can't help but serve her and love her even more. And I attempt to love her as Jesus loves the church.'

I look at Barney and how his face shines. He doesn't know it but he radiates Jesus.

I ask him one final question, 'How would you like to be remembered?'

'I'd like to be remembered for being a good daddy, a good husband and a man of God. I'm aware that I fall woefully short. But that's what I'd like to be remembered as.'

Barney could have chosen anger. He could have chosen to be bitter. He could have chosen to feel that the autumn years of his marriage have been robbed by this disease. However, after spending time with him, it is abundantly clear this is not the case. He has chosen to be a blessing, to radiate the love of God in the most trying of circumstances.

And whether he knows it or not he has chosen to rise above.

8

Out of Africa

When I first met Helen she had just returned from Tanzania after the break-up of her marriage. She reminded me of a fragile little bird, broken, but with this spirit inside her and a song in her heart that was just not going to give up.

At the time I myself was a widower, coping with the demands of two young girls without a mum, and trying to make a living as and when I could in the music industry.

Helen and I were both single, yet wary of making mistakes and so became great friends. She was the lead singer of a band that was attracting quite a lot of attention from the media. I quickly signed her to the record label for which I was acting as a consultant. Sadly, we were hampered by the politics of a large music corporation and what we'd both been working towards never realized its full potential. Our friendship did, though, and I took great delight as this charismatic (in every sense) chanteuse began to get her life back on track.

I remember quite clearly one phone conversation where I told her about this beautiful young lady I'd met and she simultaneously waxed eloquent about a handsome lawyer called

James. Within a year we were both married, and a couple of years down the line we both have two bouncing, mischievous boys.

But what had it really been like in the darkest times of Helen's life?

What had she learnt about God in the grieving process?

Helen met her first husband Paul at a drinks party at his mum's home in London and they married in 2000 when she was 29. After a wonderful honeymoon they moved straight out to Tanzania where Paul was, and still is, an exceptional wildlife and landscape photographer.

For Helen, moving to what some might consider a hostile environment was not a problem, as she'd grown up travelling the globe with her father, who was a Church of England bishop. They were married for just 18 months and, with hindsight, both knew or felt fairly quickly that they'd made the wrong decision. They were not great at communicating.

Within the first year of marriage several people close to them, on both sides of the family, died. Their huge sense of loss was compounded by a sense of isolation geographically and later emotionally. They lived in the bush, 14 miles from the nearest town, and increasingly further apart in their hearts.

Paul's business started to suffer and the two of them began to drift further and further apart. Their hearts had never really learnt to articulate their true feelings. And so they chose not to share their doubts about the marriage, even though they both wanted to make it work. It was as if they were almost prevented from doing so.

They tried hard to salvage their marriage but failed to be honest about their difficulties. As Helen put it, 'Hiding yourself is no good. Covering up is no good.'

The darkest moment came when she was hoping it would work out and then realized he didn't want it to happen.

Helen became very close to God throughout this time. She felt empty and alone and regarded the Bible as food for her soul.

'God was most clear in the darkest moments. I couldn't cope without him. I had all these beliefs that it (the marriage) could work. I was sorry about everything.'

She returned from Tanzania and went on a house party where straight away she was confronted by a verse from the Bible saying, 'Your loving kindness never fails.' She realized that it wasn't God who had let her down. We live in a sinful world and we have to choose to let God into it. She saw that God was standing with her in her pain. Even when she felt utterly deserted, he was present.

She has forgiven her husband and, likewise, he has forgiven her. However she also states that, 'Forgiveness is like an onion: there are layers. Forgiveness is a decision not a feeling.'

It would seem that we have to turn to God in a continuous cycle of repentance as we mess up, and our lives sometimes unravel, but as Helen states, 'Life is so wonderful when you're walking with God,' and even now she longs for that empty feeling again because that is when she feels closest to her creator.

I asked her how Humpty Dumpty was put back together again and she says, 'Well, the cracks will always show and that is what makes it beautiful.'

And that's it, isn't it?

We're all just cracked jars of clay, sanctified and glued together by the grace of God. Some of us are the walking wounded, but hopefully we can learn from past hurts and painful life narratives and keep moving forward towards an eternal goal.

9

He Ain't Heavy

Daniel is 53 years old. A music-business entrepreneur with George Clooney good looks, he drives a Porsche Boxster and is physically in great shape. He is married to a lovely wife called Ann and they live in Hampshire on the south coast of England.

This is his story.

My brother Pete was five years younger than me. He was the second child and was born in Canada in 1963.

We were very tight as brothers growing up. He looked like my twin, except that he was taller and very handsome, kind of like the seventies pop star David Essex.

We both attended a church in Doncaster, where the girls from the local high school went. We used to go on boys' camps and I had a basic sort of faith at this stage from spending time in this environment. I assumed Pete did too.

But we were different. He went to the local grammar school, whereas I had failed my 11-plus. He could be very funny, bordering on the outrageous, but he was also really difficult to read – nobody really knew what he was thinking. He was introverted and intensely private.

I did well and went to Oxford University where I forgot about my faith for a while. Back then, the local Christian Union was simply not the cool place to be. I had a morality though; I didn't do drugs and didn't sleep around.

I met my wife Ann there and we were exclusive from the start. The values I'd experienced at church made me live a certain way.

Pete, on the other hand, would look at girls and they would just melt. He played the field.

After completing his A levels he was meant to come to Oxford to study, but instead took a gap year and ended up in Manchester working as a trainee quantity surveyor for a building company, from which after a while he was fired. He then got a job as a bike messenger working for a record company.

I was planning to be an English teacher, until he wrote to me and said, 'There are record companies down here. You don't have to be a musician to be in the record biz.'

So I quit Oxford and got a job at CBS records in 1976. Punk was happening and it was a great time in music. A year later Pete landed a job at A&M and we shared a flat in Hampstead together and had a fantastic time.

Pete was unpredictable at times, though, and would have these enormous mood swings. He was not pleasant to be around when he did. He wouldn't ever talk or discuss how he felt. He would just have these horrible, dark moods which eventually he'd come out of.

I married Ann, who I'd first met at Oxford, and Pete more or less got married at the same time. He pretty quickly had two kids. We didn't.

I became a Christian in 1992. We led different lives but came together to play in a covers band with our younger brother Jez.

I remember one weekend we were having a big family bash and our band was playing. Pete's wife was not there. Anyway, after the gig Pete has this woman hanging off his arm as if it's the most natural thing in the world, like it was normal. Everybody at the gig was totally gobsmacked.

Pete left his wife and kids and shacked up with the new woman. The rest of the band were so hacked off they left the band, which left me and my little brother Jez trying to keep it going. It was the only contact we had with Pete.

The new woman's family had connections in the underworld and represented a lot of darkness and misery. I started praying like crazy to reach him and to be able to talk to him about his situation – trying not to judge, doing my best not to upset the family, who were incredibly angry and hurt.

A couple of years into the relationship Pete started to get into an even worse state as he began to realize his relationship with the woman was dying. His children from his marriage rejected him because he was so tough to be around. I kept praying for strength, wisdom, clarity and, yes, for love.

Pete still came to sing in the band and I kept pouring out my heart to God for my prodigal brother.

Then one day he hanged himself.

I had thought the band was enough of a lifeline to maybe try to pull him out of the blackness, but in the end he cut it.

I organized the funeral, dealt with my family and Pete's girlfriend's family, who I knew must have watched him deteriorate.

I spoke at Pete's funeral and used 1 Corinthians 13, all about love and truth.

I had a lot to deal with.

The Bible makes it clear that suicide is a sin and I had to confront the possibility that Pete might be in eternal damnation. I somehow managed to get through the funeral. I tried to point people to God, otherwise his life would have been a waste, but I think it was partly selfish on my part. I felt the girlfriend and her family were culpable. The only knowledge we have surrounding Pete's death is from them, and her brother just had something inherently disturbing about him.

They tried to avoid any blame by painting a picture of my brother as a drunk. There were factors surrounding his death which I'm just not sure about and that makes me uncomfortable. They were a criminal family and just seemed insensitive to death and suffering.

On the day of the funeral, God was in the message and the way our family members carried themselves. God showed himself at the funeral. All the people that came, apart from his girlfriend's immediate family, sat on our side of the church. It was almost like a vote against evil.

My brother left everything he had to his girlfriend – everything. He knew that his own kids would receive nothing. He made me the executor of his will. I didn't want the job, but felt it was down to me to make sure there was no skulduggery (which there was).

I wondered if Pete was trying to tell me something by this. I don't know. I do know that the will had been written several years before. Maybe Pete wrote it with the best of intentions, back in the day. So I saw it through. Afterwards, I kept myself together for everyone and didn't grieve for six months. I was carrying so much anger you could see it written all over my face. But I couldn't keep it up.

It was my wife, Ann, who eventually got two mates to sit me down and talk it out. They said, 'You need to deal with this,' at which point I lost it. I finally let the emotion out.

My vicar was fantastic with me: we prayed and went through Scripture together and I felt stronger. I prayed with my family, (they're not all Christians). My brother Jez started going to church.

But I struggled. Had I prayed inaccurately? Maybe I should have been bolder, more pro-active? Was it right to pray and wait? I'd always looked out for Pete. I said to myself, 'Where is he at the end of this? What has happened to him? Did he just get so low that he wanted to bail out on everybody?' I was also angry with him because of his kids. They lost him twice. Once when he left them and once again when he hung himself. I was angry because of the pain he caused my mum and dad.

Then I also thought, well, God loves him. I was also challenged to think about who really is a Christian and who isn't. And one day it came to me. Jesus on the cross had two criminals beside him and one of them asked Jesus to remember him.

Jesus did not at that point say, 'Repent of your sins,' or 'Just believe.'

He simply said, 'Today you will be with me in paradise' (Luke 23:43).

He'd recognized a change of heart in the man next to him. That is all he needed to know.

So then, how long does it take, when you kick the stool away and you're dangling on a dead man's rope, to realize that you've gone too far?

How long does it take a man to realize he's done wrong, to repent of his sins and give himself to God?

If a change of heart is required, that can be in a split second.

So how do I know Pete didn't do that?

God's criteria count, not ours.

So I cling to that, because to contemplate the alternative would mean that God did not answer my prayers, and I prayed constantly for Pete.

I could not believe he wouldn't answer my prayer for one of his children and leave Pete confined to eternal damnation.

The Bible tells us to pray with the right attitude.

I believe God answered my prayer. Pete got to where he was by making some bad choices, but he was not an evil man.

And who doesn't make bad choices?

That's why we need a Saviour.

Reflecting on Daniel's story it occurs to me that Daniel and his family endured a number of tragic losses.

First, there was the loss of trust, when he brazenly turned up to a gig with another woman on his arm.

Then there was the loss for his wife and children when Pete deserted them.

There was also the loss of the Pete they used to know and grew up with.

Finally, there was the loss of Pete's life, so jagged and final.

What can we take that might be positive from this story?

Well, I think we see a very strong commitment to honour God and the memory of his late brother from Daniel. It's in the detail of how he relates the story and what happens at the funeral, and later over the will.

The bigger picture, which Daniel is too modest to tell you about, is how he has lived his life out since then. He is one of life's quiet servants. He sees a need and, though it may only be for a season, he is faithful and completes the journey. There is no way I could ever sugarcoat what is without doubt a tragedy, but neither Daniel nor his younger brother Jez have let it ruin their lives. They have had the courage to learn from the pain and keep going, and I admire them both immensely.

10

The Lonely Hearts Club

I met Jerry in Warwick at a Christian Vision for Men conference where I was speaking. He came up to me afterwards and told me his wife Pauline had just been diagnosed with cancer. I decided there and then to be his buddy and journey the miles with him. He was in his mid-50s with his boys both grown up and looking forward to having more time to relax. At that point he reminded me of a big, sweet, angry bear of a man: feisty, but determined; hurt, but not about to throw in the towel.

A little while later, I drove down to Portsmouth to see Jerry and meet his wife Pauline. She was obviously seriously ill, but beautiful and defiant with it.

The visit was made a little bizarre, as while driving down to meet them, the Jeremy Vine Show had rung and said they wanted me to do a phone interview.

I politely explained that this might not be possible but I'd see when I got to Jerry and Pauline's house. They, God bless them, thought this was very funny and graciously allowed me to duck out for ten minutes while they listened to the broadcast in their lounge.

Pauline had that glow about her that I have seen in a lot of very ill people. It is almost angelic, like somehow a small cloud of God's presence is hanging over them helping them cope.

Jerry was struggling and it reminded me of my own journey nearly ten years ago. He felt that everything was out of control and there was nothing to do except pray.

Over the next few months we stayed in touch, and as Pauline's health deteriorated I suggested they try to go on a cruise to celebrate life, enjoy new experiences and create memories. This they did and had a wonderful time. I've seen the photographs and they both look happy and radiant.

A few short months later I drove down again. It was apparent Pauline's cancer had progressed significantly and there was little time left.

With Jerry and Pauline's permission I sat with them and gently stroked Pauline's forehead and prayed for her. That day when I travelled home I did not put the radio on as I normally would, but instead drove in silence with tears rolling down my face.

I was crying because I knew exactly what was coming next.

Sure enough, it wasn't long before I got the call from Jerry.

Pauline had passed from this life to the next.

At the funeral I watched as her mortal body was laid in the ground, witnessed the bravery of their sons and watched as Jerry was left on his own to say his last goodbyes.

That has to be one of the loneliest moments in life.

Finally we hugged and I welcomed him to the club that nobody wants to join.

A few years on and Jerry has discovered a new life and has been brave enough to embrace it. His heart has been softened by what he has endured and he is tackling life head on and enjoying it.

Both his sons are now married and life is good.

As for Jerry he might even get married again one day too . . . who knows?

What he does know is that God was there in the mess by his side and that by faith and the grace of God he has endured.

11

Heartbreak Ridge

Every Saturday night at 8 p.m., courtesy of Premier Christian Radio, you can hear me on your digital radio or television talking to a varied bunch of people, from pop stars to politicians, charity workers to comedians, Hollywood stars and wannabes to people like you and me – normal people (well relatively!) who have a story to tell about what life has sometimes harshly dealt them and they have tried to endure.

Pete and Susannah are a handsome, young married couple in their early thirties who are no strangers to heartbreak. The following is a transcript of my interview with them.

NICK: Welcome to the programme Pete and Susannah. You have had a unique journey. You look to me like you're in your late twenties or early thirties. You look fresh-faced and young, compared to my good self!

PETER: We're in our early thirties.

NICK: And yet I read a fascinating article about what's happened to you in your life and in your marriage. Where do we begin with that?

PETER: I think the way I begin to talk about it is to say we've had quite a lot of exposure to the death of babies, both late in pregnancy and shortly after birth. My wife can maybe talk about each of the children and the different circumstances, but it felt as though, when we'd had the miscarriage of one baby, that after that experience we went through more trials – as if God was bit by bit exposing us to deeper forms of death and pain around the birth of children that we loved.

NICK: I don't know what the statistics are for miscarriage. Is it one in four?

SUSANNAH: Yes, one in four pregnancies result in early miscarriage, late miscarriage or stillbirth.

We found out we were expecting our first child shortly after I'd lost my mother, in 2008. The pregnancy progressed pretty normally and, shortly after we were about 21 weeks, we went for our '20 week' scan. I had been concerned about movement for a while. At that point it was confirmed that our baby had died in the womb. We usually talk about it in terms of stillbirth although technically anything before 24 weeks is a late miscarriage. Obviously, at that stage, you actually have to give birth and have your baby. So we had a boy called Calvin on 8 January 2009.

NICK: Those kinds of days are carved on your heart, aren't they? How do you start to get over that and want to have another child again? I think it would take a great deal of bravery on both your parts. Also, how do you find unity as a couple when it is such an individual and yet shared journey?

PETER: I think we both experienced the grief and the loss in different ways. I found myself experiencing deep, sickening pain and grief at two particular moments that stand out in my memory.

First of all, in the two or so days after being told that Calvin had died in the womb, I had to go home and wait a couple of days before seeing him and spending some moments with him.

They were really agonizing – long, drawn out days. They felt like they lasted an eternity. And then, when we could actually see him and hold him, knowing that he'd already gone to be with the Lord, there were just waves of sickening grief and pain.

Susannah, I think you shared that, but had other feelings at this time?

SUSANNAH: It is a very unreal time and when we went to have him, at that point we didn't know it was a boy. I actually didn't want the baby to be a boy, because before Pete and I had even met, we'd both had the same favourite boy's name. We'd discussed this, as couples tend to, in preparation for marriage, and long before we got married we decided that if we had a boy we'd call him Calvin. We even had a cat that we called Hobbes after Calvin and Hobbes, the famous cartoon. And we had Hobbes at home waiting for a little boy Calvin to come back.

When they said the baby had died, and then after we had him and realized it was a boy, we felt it was another blow. How did we go on to have another child after that? I think we just trusted God.

When you leave the hospital, your arms ache for the child that you don't have. The sight of pregnant women is very difficult – the sight of newborn babies too. I remember one time in Sainsbury's, I was pushing a trolley and this lady had a newborn baby. I think it was around Calvin's due date. It was just how I imagined Calvin to be and I kept passing her in every aisle. By the time I got to the last aisle I almost wanted to pick up the baby and run. I felt slightly crazy.

We were strong Christians. Pete, at the time, was training to be a minister and we gave our grief to God and felt that if God could bring us through this, he could bring us through another pregnancy. Even if we lost another baby he would be faithful to us, so we continued to hope for another baby and we were fortunate, I guess, to find we were pregnant quite quickly after that.

NICK: So how soon after that did you conceive again?

SUSANNAH: We actually found out I was pregnant with our son, Lewis, the day after Calvin's due date. Yes, pretty quickly really. It was quite a shock.

That pregnancy progressed normally, although they scanned me a lot more frequently, until Christmas Day 2009 (the same calendar year). We went to church that morning and I hadn't felt the baby move for a while and I thought, 'That's a little bit odd.' The music at church didn't get the baby moving. We went home and had Christmas lunch, which didn't get him moving. I ate an entire chocolate orange, which didn't get him moving, at which point I said we needed to get to the hospital.

We went in and, thankfully, his heartbeat was fine but kept dipping. They monitored me for several hours, and then, just before Boxing Day morning they said they needed to deliver him.

He arrived safely, with the cord wrapped tightly round his neck, five weeks early. Thankfully he's well and keeps us on our toes.

He's now 4.

NICK: What a hard road for such a young couple to take. So Lewis is alive and well, a robust 4-year-old?

BOTH: Yes.

PETER: He's enthusiastic – a happy chap. He woke me up at 6.30 this morning.

NICK: So a big old journey, but I guess a real celebration when he came along and a really wonderful, wonderful time?

SUSANNAH: Yes, obviously he was early, so he had to stay in hospital a little bit longer than most babies, but we couldn't believe he was here and that he was well and coming home.

NICK: Then you fell pregnant again?

SUSANNAH: Yes, we waited a couple of years before we ventured into trying for another baby. In September 2012 we miscarried twins at an early stage – nine weeks. That was another sadness, but thankfully I quite quickly fell pregnant again. So now it was my fourth pregnancy and this one started fine: the sickness kicked in early and I was feeling as I should be – exhausted, sick, but really encouraged.

We were heading quickly towards Christmas at this point, and around the start of Advent (I would have been eight or nine weeks) I started to notice that I wasn't feeling sick like I normally would have been at this point in the pregnancy. So I started to develop nagging doubts in the back of my mind that something wasn't quite right. But it was Advent, so we pressed on with getting ready for Christmas at Latimer College where we were living.

Pete was curate of the church at the time and we were pretty busy teaching our little boy all about Jesus' birth and what Christmas is really about, trying to counter all the big messages he was getting from pre-school regarding Santa

Claus. So we put it to the back of our minds. Our 12 week scan was scheduled for 28 December, so we cracked on with Christmas and I tried not to worry.

We went for our 12 week scan and sat in that waiting room. I'll never forget it, being with all these other excited pregnant ladies who couldn't wait to see their babies on the screen. I remember saying to Pete, 'You know I'm really not sure about this. It feels a lot more like the twins we've just lost than it does Calvin and Lewis, who at 12 weeks were perfectly normal.'

We were called in and I hopped up onto the couch and the lady started the scan. Immediately I noticed on the screen that the baby was quite still, whereas normally the baby would have been moving.

I said to Pete, 'Oh, looks a bit still,' and she zoomed in straightaway and said, 'There's the heartbeat; baby's alive.' So we had two minutes of real joy. Wow, this is really happening! In July we're having a baby. Not a great time of the year to have a baby, but I made my peace with that in the two minutes. All was going to be fine and I was really excited.

Then we noticed the stenographer was really quiet, and she turned the screen away from us.

We asked, 'Is everything OK?'

She said, 'I just need to do a few more measurements.'

While she kept measuring I felt this sinking feeling, that this wasn't good. She said, 'Um . . . baby's head is just measuring a little small for what I would expect at this stage of gestation.'

The baby was only measuring about 10 weeks and I knew I was 12, so we knew at that point something was wrong.

Then she left us to go and get the doctor and tears started to roll down our faces as we realized it really can't be good at 12 weeks for the baby's head to be measuring wrong. We didn't have any idea what that meant, but we did know the baby was most likely super-poorly.

PETER: After a while we spoke to some of the specialists, and there was an expectation from them that we would terminate the pregnancy because they told us there was no hope: 'Your baby is alive now but will die very soon.'

I didn't like the idea of feeling pressured into that. I don't believe that we as people have the right to end a pregnancy in the womb. I think that's really God's decision. So I was very unhappy about that and demanded some more information.

As we began to get more information we found out that our baby had anencephaly, which means the brain wasn't going to develop and that the baby wouldn't be able to live. But it was also clear that when mothers carry on with the pregnancy many of these babies live for a time after birth, not feeling pain or anything; they just live for a while and then die.

So we took the decision to carry on with the pregnancy.

We went through the whole pregnancy with Susannah doing all the normal things and us coming to love the child, and talking to our 3-year-old boy about the baby, while knowing that actually it was going to end in a death . . .

SUSANNAH: The pressure to abort was quite high and the medical staff were making claims that we discovered afterwards were perhaps untrue. The fact is that in most cases these babies are aborted – that's why they don't survive to birth . . .

NICK: That's a lot of pressure for a young couple to have . . .

SUSANNAH: Yeah . . .

NICK: So what happened?

SUSANNAH: Well, back in the waiting room when we were told the baby had anencephaly and wouldn't survive, we were desperately trying to come to terms with that and yet we were also aware that we had to come to a decision quickly. The doctors didn't actually use the term 'abort' or 'terminate'. They said, 'We can resolve matters here. You don't need to go to see a specialist, we will just resolve things. We'll get the paperwork ...' In fact, they came in with the paperwork for us to sign ready for an abortion. Through sheer determination we said, 'Hold on, the baby's alive. We need to have a clear understanding of what's going on and what the implications are before we do anything.' We made it quite clear we didn't want to abort.

I remember sitting in the room and I just crumpled in on myself and closed my eyes, drew my arms up to my chest as I cried and sobbed, and said:

'My first baby, Calvin, he changed me. I'm a stronger person because I had him. My relationship with God is better because I had him. I learnt so much in those dark times that actually, I'm grateful I had him. He changed me and I love him for that. This baby's going to change me too . . . so I want to get to know him or her. I want to go through this pregnancy.'

I remember in the back of my head a little song came into my mind that I'd learnt as a child:

> Trust and obey,
> For there's no other way
> To be happy in Jesus,
> But to trust and obey.*

Trust and Obey lyrics by John H. Sammis, 1887.

And it felt to us that the obedient path was not to question God's sovereignty or take a decision for ourselves, but just to have this baby – this baby he'd given us. For the good of our marriage we would have him or her, get to know him or her for as long as the baby was in our family.

We left that hospital realizing that I was going to continue to grow, that people were going to keep asking me, 'When's your baby due?' and, 'Are you having a girl or a boy?'

NICK: And any one of those is like a dagger to your heart.

SUSANNAH: Absolutely. It's really tough. And sometimes I got it wrong. To complete strangers, I'd say, 'Well actually, my baby's going to die.' And I would think afterwards that maybe that wasn't the most sensitive or appropriate thing to say . . .

NICK: But you're dealing with very difficult stuff – it's the day-to-day almost flippant stuff, the casual remarks that people make, that's really quite piercing. They don't mean to be; it's unintentional.

PETER: We were trying to love the baby as best we could and to give her the best life we could. We knew it would be short. It would be mainly in the womb.

As it turns out, she was born. She lived for 80 minutes in our arms after birth, and those 80 minutes were really wonderful. We were doing everything we could to love and care for her. Our little boy, Lewis, was able to come in and meet his sister in the hospital. He remembers that – the little soft toys for him to give her and for her to give him. He keeps his by his bed. He talks about her.

Other little children that know about Anastasia (this is what we named her), and are friends with Lewis, have said things like, 'Can I ask Jesus to give Anastasia a cuddle for me, 'cos I can't cuddle her.' It's really sweet to see a 4-year-old child talking about heaven and about God loving a little baby like that. It's absolutely beautiful. Tragic, but . . . such beauty and love at the centre of all that pain.

Both Susannah and I would say we wouldn't want any of it to have been any other way and we'd go through it again. The sadness doesn't go away but there is joy in the midst of sadness and you can't have it any other way.

SUSANNAH: We had the unusual experience of two paths placed before us – the path of suffering or the path which had a seemingly quick and easy resolution (although in reality I think it would have been suffering in another way). We chose the path that was frightening and the path which we were terrified to take, and couldn't imagine how we'd cope. The thing that surprised us, and blew us away really, was just how much joy God brought to us through that experience, and through the love we received from other Christians at the college where we were living. The student body were really supportive and brilliant. Our church family was great, and friends near and far too . . .

I wrote a blog, a private blog for our friends and family to keep updated, and we received love and support from all around the world.

And the pregnancy itself brought real joy. We treasured Anastasia's movements more. I think we took things for granted with previous pregnancies. This time we bought lots of different things that we could turn into keepsakes during the time we knew we would have with Anastasia at the hospital. It was really joyful.

NICK: And did you take photographs and things like that?

SUSANNAH: Yes, we planned two weeks before she eventually arrived. Ten weeks early my bump had got to such a size that I thought, 'Let's get some professional photos taken – a maternity shoot.' So we had a family shoot with a lovely lady who works for a charity called Now I Lay Me Down to Sleep. They come into hospitals if your baby's been stillborn and they'll take some professional photos of your baby. So we discussed with her the possibility of her coming to the birth because we didn't know how long we'd get and we wanted photos of her while she was alive. She came to the entire birth and photographed everything.

NICK: What an amazing lady.

SUSANNAH: Yes, she was so kind.

PETER: After we took the decision to love Anastasia and to carry through to term, we were transferred over to the specialist hospital at UCL in London. The team of doctors there were amazing and hugely supportive: they are doing truly pioneering work with babies in the womb and they did everything they could to love and care for Anastasia in a kind way. It was very moving to be on the receiving end of care that went beyond just medical attention. We all knew the situation we were in. There was no way this baby's brain was going to grow back any more than your arm would grow back if you cut it off. But they understood our desire to love her and they respected it and they helped us in all kinds of ways. It was great.

NICK: Did you continue praying for miracles?

SUSANNAH: I think another thing that really surprised us was that right from the moment of that 12 week scan, I never thought Anastasia was going to live, and actually I think it would have been disobedient for us to ask for her to live. I had such a peace that she was going to die at that time, and that this was the path God had chosen for her.

A number of friends contacted us and said, 'We're really praying for a miracle.' They were taken aback when I replied, 'Thank you so much, but please pray for our peace, for our joy; I really think that's the miracle God's going to do here. I don't think she's going to live.'

PETER: There are other situations where we have wanted to pray for a miracle and have seen that, but this time it didn't feel right.

NICK: What about the future?

PETER: I think one of the great things that we've found as we've trusted God with our suffering is that, as we read in 2 Corinthians chapter 1, the comfort that God gives us is then used to comfort other people. We found that we were comforted greatly by the ministry of a couple in America called Nancy and David Guthrie who experienced child loss themselves. They run retreats for parents who have lost children at any stage of life, not just young children but older children as well, from anything – cancer, violence, accidents. We thought we'd love to go on one of their retreats for couples. So we got the money together to go. But then we thought, 'Why don't we fly them over and do a retreat here instead?'

NICK: Bless more people.

PETER: So that's what we've done.

SUSANNAH: When you lose a child it's there forever. You never expect to outlive your children.

NICK: No, it's not the natural order of things. It's not how it should be.

PETER: It would be great if churches were known as places where people who are hurt, struggling and suffering can come and find a warm welcome.

NICK: Forgive me asking this, but do you have a desire to have any more children?

SUSANNAH: I think that would be lovely if the Lord blesses us in that way. We've always said that we look at Lewis and he's such a joy, that he's worth all the heartache, and in fact even if we have more heartache, God has taught us so much, that we would go through it again in a heartbeat. It's a privilege to be able to fall pregnant and have children.

All the time I was going through this my sister-in-law in America was struggling with the fact that she couldn't even conceive, and I know the heartache in that. It is a real joy and a blessing to have children, even for a short time. You wouldn't trade that for anything.

PETER: There's a great misunderstanding in this country that Christianity is simply about believing certain truths, just getting on with life and fitting these beliefs into your life. In reality it's much more beautiful than that. It's opening your life to God and other people, and doing that inevitably involves suffering. But the thing is, holding back involves a worse kind of suffering. So absolutely we'd be keen to have more children, and whatever it is God has in store for us, we'll trust him.'

NICK: Peter and Susannah, thank you so much for coming in and sharing and for being so vulnerable and faithful.

May the Lord bless you, guide you, keep you and all your children, in Jesus' name. Amen.

BOTH: Thank you very much.

Peter and Susannah leave.

NICK: What a precious couple, what a very special programme and what a privilege it is in my job to be alongside people like that. I hope you've enjoyed it. I hope you've been moved, and I hope you've drawn closer to God through this past hour.

Courtesy of Premier Christian Radio:
Transcript of an interview first broadcast Saturday 29 March 2014.

The Brightest of Stars

Life is full of bright stars and one of them was married to my good friend Malcolm Down. Her name was Dawn, and from the first time I met her, on the night of my fiftieth birthday, I knew she was a real character – feisty, fun-loving and someone who, like me, called a spade a shovel. At that point she was six years into her cancer journey.

I'd met Malcolm when he had kindly agreed to publish my first book *Big Boys Don't Cry* and we had an immediate connection because of my first wife, Lynn's, cancer story. That was in 2007 and I have to say we have been and remain firm friends.

Dawn had a passion for music and the arts and also for equipping young people through the magic and mystery of it. She started a charity called Spectrum Arts and helped hundreds of children over the years. I have met maybe a handful of women who had the 'life force' that she did and I liked her immensely.

Throughout Dawn's cancer journey Malcolm, like many men before him, put her needs before his own as he watched her wither away, while also caring for their three children. It is perhaps no accident that he likes to run marathons and indeed is one of the fastest men in his age bracket. What he had to endure with Dawn was just that – long, painful, drawn out – a marathon of endurance. You have to be fit to survive that, emotionally and spiritually.

Dawn continued to teach the piano whenever she could. There were numerous fundraisers for Spectrum Arts. These meant that when a child could not afford the fees, they would regularly waive them in order to give someone an opportunity who really needed it. She was brilliant at motivating kids whom other people would call, to put it politely, challenging.

As in life, when it came to her illness Dawn wasn't afraid to take risks, and through vigorous fundraising and a few more marathons run by Malcolm, when funds allowed, she would fly to Mexico to the Oasis of Hope Hospital – an alternative holistic cancer treatment centre run by Dr Francisco Contreras.

A while back I had the privilege of interviewing Malcolm about his life and journey and here is what he had to say.

NICK: Tell the listeners something about yourself because when I first met you, you were about to embark on a journey I'd already travelled.

MALCOLM: Well yes, we met at a period in my life when my wife Dawn had been diagnosed with ovarian cancer. I think at that point she was probably in the latter stages of her life. She'd been diagnosed back in 2001 with stage-three ovarian cancer so it was already quite serious and normally life expectancy for people with stage three is about two years. So the prognosis wasn't very good and we obviously went through a rollercoaster of emotions. Dawn went through all the National Health options such as chemotherapy. She lost her hair and, being the sort of person that she was – a real fighter – she decided she would fight the disease in an alternative way, which resulted in her seeking treatment at The Oasis of Hope Hospital in Mexico. I firmly believe that her life was extended because of the treatment she received there, way beyond the years that the NHS gave her. In fact she ended up living for nine years. All but the last year, really, she spent in reasonable health and we were able to enjoy some incredible times while the family was still growing up. I just give thanks to God for the times we had.

NICK: She was an extraordinary character. She was larger than life.

MALCOLM: She was . . .

NICK: As I remember, she was a woman not to be trifled with . . .

MALCOLM: (Laughs) Absolutely . . . woe betide any man that tried!

NICK: But she was also a greatly creative person. She played the piano. She taught at the creative arts school she founded . . .

MALCOLM: That's right. She was a piano teacher and at any one time would be teaching up to forty pupils. She'd put on regular concerts for those pupils and then she started Spectrum Arts in 2005 with her friend Andrea Louise. It's a performing arts workshop run over the Easter and summer holidays, giving kids who enjoy the performing arts an opportunity to have a go, no matter what their background might be. It was my promise to her the day before she died that I would try to keep it going. So Spectrum Arts is still going, I'm pleased to say.

NICK: How long is it since Dawn passed?

MALCOLM: It was 2010, so four-and-a-half years now.

NICK: What has been the hardest thing on your journey with Dawn?

MALCOLM: Very good question . . . I think trying to be strong for the children's sake was probably the hardest thing because there was this internal conflict going on the whole time. Inside I was falling apart because I knew my wife was dying . . . especially towards the end . . . but I didn't want to let the children see what I was going through . . . so I felt that I had to put a really brave face on for them the whole time, and put as much positive spin on the illness as possible because they were very young at the time. My youngest, Sarah, was only 7 when Dawn was diagnosed. I've got two other children: Hayley, who was 11, and David, who was 9 at the time . . . so they spent their teenage years with their mum being ill and that was tough for them, especially when Hayley went away to university and wasn't around as much. That was particularly hard.

NICK: Yes, it's that sense of impending loss, isn't it? And Hayley going away was a loss as well. It's hard for whoever's left to shoulder the burden while the partner's alive. It's very hard because you're in the process of burying all your needs yourself whilst managing other people's expectations, which can include your partner's parents, your children, your friends, your church, all that stuff. It's a very complex minefield to tiptoe through. Dawn fought very bravely and courageously and when she died I wonder if, like me with Lynn, you felt a strange sense of guilty release?

MALCOLM: That's probably a really good way of expressing it. When you have lived with someone who's been through cancer, it is a long journey in a lot of cases, and you live it every day. The disease doesn't go away. Even though she went through periods of relatively good health, where we could put it to the back of our minds, it was always there in the background somewhere. So you live with the thing every day of your lives, and you see the agony that your closest friend, your dearly beloved, goes through, especially towards the end, and you really wouldn't want to wish that on your worst enemy. Anyone who knows what it is like to live with someone who's gone through the final stages of cancer will know what I'm talking about. I don't want to go into too much detail, but it must be one of the most horrific things to watch someone whom you love go through. So when she did finally pass away, yes, there was a sense of relief that you no longer have to . . . do the daily injections. You no longer have to look after all of the other needs there are . . .

NICK: And it is tricky isn't it? Because we weren't brought up to be nurses yet we had to be nurses and carers, and flush out veins at strange times of the day and do all the kind of bathing stuff, and to see these glorious women slowly ebb away in front of our eyes . . .

MALCOLM: And obviously you're devastated with the loss, at the time of death, and my heart was broken – in the same way that anyone who has lost a partner would be – and you go into shock. Some of the body's defences kick in. God has created an amazing thing with the human body and it does extraordinary things sometimes. He gave me . . . I know he gave me the ability to get through those first few weeks in a supernatural way. I still look back to this day and think about those first few weeks and I just wonder how I got through them, but somehow I did . . .

NICK: Where were your friends and family? And church in all this grief?

MALCOLM: Well they were there, obviously . . . I was busy trying to be strong for the children, but they were a tremendous support to me. I remember I didn't sleep much the first night after she passed away. We all slept in one room. Bizarrely, we watched a DVD at three o'clock in the morning because none of us could sleep and it seemed the only thing we could do to help pass the time. We did finally get to sleep and when we woke up in the morning we all just went for a walk and took the dog out. It was a unique time of bonding for the family, around that whole sense of shared grief, and Dawn, in her wisdom, knew that we would need some time away as a family, so she actually encouraged us to go. One of her last wishes was that we would go away on a family holiday and so we booked, within a few weeks of her death, a holiday to Florida to visit all the theme parks. That was an amazing time.

NICK: I can imagine. It would be weird because 'she's not there', but at the same time, you are all in it together. It was the Down family versus the world with God on your side.

MALCOLM: Yes, and because I think we had that really close bonding time we drew strength from one another, because we each knew what the other was feeling. My kids are exceptional. My daughter Sarah was going through GCSEs at the time her mum died and she still came out with six A-stars and has gone on to university now. I think, how did you do that?! My eldest daughter was at university – she came out with a first. My son got distinctions in his college exams and is now training to be a sports therapist. You see so many other children whose lives seem to be wrecked after the death of a parent. I'm just so grateful that my kids seem to have come through it somehow.

NICK: Well, they've got a very special dad.

MALCOLM: I don't know about that!

NICK: When you're thrown into the fiery pit like that, you do grow close together and there is this sense that we can never be Mum as well, but we do have to double up on everything.

MALCOLM: Absolutely, well I try to do that (laughs). I may not be the best judge of how successful I've been.

NICK: What has life been like for you since then? And what is life like now for the children?

MALCOLM: Gosh, good question. It's been four years now. I think in the early days you just get used to a different way of life. You talked earlier about that sense of relief almost, but also the devastation of not having your partner in your life any more, so the immediate months afterwards, as you well know, are a period of adjustment. You are now a widower. You are now single.

NICK: That's strange in itself . . .

MALCOLM: It is. I was married for 24 years and you're used to relating to the world as a married person. Then all of a sudden you're not. That brings all sorts of challenges. Little things, like my wedding ring – I didn't take it off for two years afterwards because I still felt married. I wasn't prepared to accept the title of single person; I didn't even know what that felt like any more. So there was a period of adjustment and it probably took me a long time. About a year after Dawn passed away I started dating an old friend. It was a long-distance relationship and we didn't see an awful lot of each other, but the good thing about it was that I did have someone to talk to who knew Dawn, who was one of her best friends. We spent a lot of time on the phone. She'd lost her dad and knew something about grief, and I think it actually really helped to have someone who I could just pick up the phone and chat things through with at any time. Although the relationship didn't work out, I am really grateful for having that person in my life.

NICK: It's funny you should say that because quite often, possibly because of the grief, men in particular will perhaps go into another relationship quicker than women will. And the thing we miss is not the physical as much as being heard, having somebody to talk to. I think at that stage we are very vulnerable.

MALCOLM: Yes, when I found myself back in the dating game I suddenly realized all the rules had changed. I felt like a fish out of water. We didn't have texts or emails or social media back in the day, so my interpretation of various things was completely different from the way things were intended.

NICK: It's hard to navigate these emotional waters. It's a tricky business isn't it?

MALCOLM: Yes it is, but for now I'm perfectly content. I don't feel like I'm missing out. I have a very full and active life.

The thing I love about Malcolm's story is his love for his family, how he endured, along with his late wife Dawn, the rigours of the cancer, and how he somehow, by the grace of

God, found the strength to carry on after she died. His love for his children and evident pride in them is also wonderful to witness. Possibly because he is such an able athlete, he has developed a disciplined approach to his life and work – one that continues to work really well for him. Above all else he has clung to the cross with tremendous courage through the darkest of times and, like me, he believes that there is always hope.

Dawn was a bright star, but she would be immensely proud of just how brightly Malcolm and the family continue to shine.

It is, perhaps, her greatest legacy.

Never give up.

Hope remains.

Epilogue

At the start of this book I wrote about loss and about how we can win. I could write lots of bland epithets and platitudes about how it is all going to be all right. In a sense it *is* all going to be all right, just not in the way you might imagine. The accounts you have just read of how these lovely people dealt with love, loss and loneliness are inspiring, but I would be doing all of us a disservice if I didn't recount some of the harder things you have to work through. It is a long journey. The winning is a daily thing. It's in smelling the coffee, smiling more, learning patience, dying to self even when you want to throttle somebody, letting things go. As Richard Carlson titled his bestselling book: *Don't Sweat the Small Stuff.*[*]

The truth is I am very good at writing and giving you all advice but absolutely rubbish at doing it!

For example, I unknowingly carried the grief and loss for my first wife into my second marriage with Nicky. I didn't mean to, it just happened. Thank God I married the right woman. She had the strength, forthrightness and grace to deal

---

[*]Richard Carlson, *Don't Sweat the Small Stuff* (London: Hodder & Stoughton, 1998).

with me when I couldn't see the wood for the trees. It must be hard to marry into an existing family where the partner died young and was a pillar of the local church and community, lauded by some, missed by many – where there are young children desperate for love but missing their mum, and where the husband is still wrestling with God over unresolved issues in regard to justice and fairness.

And let's not get started on the bloke in the armchair wallowing in a glass of wine.

As Nicky often says, the children were easy in comparison to me.

My poor wife!

Ten years in now and I'm getting there. We, thank God, are getting there.

I'm not looking to air dirty laundry here but just to be real with you all. We are all works in progress, especially when we're trying to work out the really hard stuff.

The last thing I wanted to do was to write a book of triumphalistic stories, when the reality is a lot more bloody and awkward. All the people whose accounts you have read have had to journey through the most awful times, but sometimes that's just the deal. Bad things happen to good people, and if I've said this once in my life I've said it a thousand times.

How we respond to tragedy and pain in our life is a matter of character and integrity. It is what shapes us and refines us.

And life and faith for me are all about integrity.

If we lose that, we have lost everything.

I hope that somewhere in here you may have glimpsed that and been encouraged in the process.

Gravel Road Trust

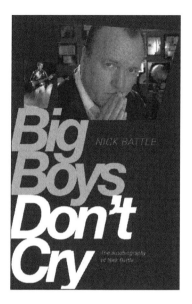

Big Boys Don't Cry

The autobiography of Nick Battle

The true story of Nick Battle, former bass guitarist with 80s Christian rock band After the Fire, who became a music industry mogul.

Personal tragedy and triumph are never far from Nick as he journeys through life trying to balance his faith with the self-obsessed industry in which he works.

Following great success working with such famous names as the Spice Girls, Cliff Richard, Talking Heads, Clannad and Take That, Nick's life suddenly changes dramatically because of a family crisis.

Discover how Nick has to give up a six-figure salary but in the process experiences God's love in a new and living way and learns how to trust God completely when everything else seems to be going wrong.

978-1-86024-612-8

The Daily Male

Nick Battle

The Daily Male breathes the fresh air of common sense and biblical faith into men's often stifled discipleship. More than forty different subjects are looked at in bite-sized chunks including fitness, fatherhood, anxiety, over-eating, over-drinking, Mondays, fidelity, vision, heroes and recycling.

Nick is on a mission to tell it like it is and will probably make you laugh out loud in the process.

978-1-86024-702-6

The Daily Male 2

Nick Battle

The Daily Male 2 provides a second helping of wit and wisdom from the author, musician and broadcaster Nick Battle. As ever, he pulls no punches. All manner of issues are explored: mothers, motorbikes, pubs, prayer, buggies, bankers, grace, dentists, desire, critics . . . and even your daughter's boyfriend.

This is not a book for the faint-hearted, but for real men with real issues and real faith, boldly trying to work out where God is in the twenty-first century.

978-1-86024-767-5